BY NAOKI HIGASHIDA

*Fall Down 7 Times Get Up 8*
*The Reason I Jump*

FALL
DOWN
7 TIMES | GET
UP 8

# FALL DOWN 7 TIMES GET UP 8

## A YOUNG MAN'S VOICE FROM THE SILENCE OF AUTISM

### NAOKI HIGASHIDA

TRANSLATED BY
**K A YOSHIDA**
AND **DAVID MITCHELL**

RANDOM HOUSE
NEW YORK

*q\7*

Published in the United States by Random House, an imprint
and division of Penguin Random House LLC, New York.

RANDOM HOUSE and the HOUSE colophon are registered
trademarks of Penguin Random House LLC.

LIBRARY OF CONGRESS CATALOGING-IN-PUBLICATION DATA
Names: Higashida, Naoki, author.
Title: Fall down 7 times get up 8 : a young man's voice from the
silence of autism / Naoki Higashida ;
translated by KA Yoshida and David Mitchell.
Other titles: Fall down seven times get up eight
Description: First edition. | New York : Random House, [2017]
Identifiers: LCCN 2017004105 | ISBN 9780812997392 (hardback) |
ISBN 9780812997408 (ebook)
Subjects: LCSH: Higashida, Naoki, 1992– —Health. | Autistic
people—Japan—Biography. | Autistic people—Psychology. |
Autism. | BISAC: BIOGRAPHY & AUTOBIOGRAPHY /
Medical. | PSYCHOLOGY / Psychopathology / Autism
Spectrum Disorders.
Classification: LCC RC553.A88 H52 2017 |
DDC 616.85/8820092 [B]—dc23
LC record available at lccn.loc.gov/2017004105

Printed in the United States of America
on acid-free paper

randomhousebooks.com

9 8 7 6 5 4 3 2 1

FIRST EDITION

*Book design by Simon M. Sullivan*

# CONTENTS

はい ◎ 取消し ✕ いいえ

Q W E R T Y U I O P

A S D F G H J K L

Z X C V B N M ?

0 1 2 3 4 5 6 7 8 9 10

田「」( )行 田 おわり

# INTRODUCTION
## DAVID MITCHELL

Naoki Higashida is an amiable and thoughtful young man now in his early twenties who lives with his family in Chiba, a prefecture adjacent to Tokyo. Naoki has autism of a type labeled severe and nonverbal, so a free-flowing conversation of the kind that facilitates the lives of most of us is impossible for him. By dint of training, stamina and patience, however, he has learned to communicate by "typing out" sentences on an alphabet grid—a QWERTY keyboard layout drawn on a sheet of card with an added "YES," "NO" and "FINISHED." Naoki voices the phonetic characters of the Japanese *hiragana* alphabet as he touches the corresponding Roman letters and builds up sentences, which a transcriber takes down. (Nobody else's hand is near Naoki's during this process, a point that alphabet-grid communicators in a skeptical world need to restate ad infinitum.) If this sounds like an arduous way to get your meaning across, you're right, it is; in addition, Naoki's autism bombards him with distractions and prompts him to get up mid-sentence, pace the room and gaze out of the window. He is easily ejected from his train of thought and forced to begin the sentence again. I've watched Naoki produce a complex sentence within sixty seconds, but I've also seen him take twenty minutes to complete a line of just a few words. By writing on a laptop Naoki can dispense with the human transcriber, but the screen and the text-converter (the drop-down menus required for writing Japanese) add a new layer of distraction. It was via his alphabet grid or his computer keyboard that Naoki wrote every sentence in this book.

I met Naoki's writing before I met Naoki. My son has autism and my wife is from Japan, so when our boy was very young and his autism at its most grimly challenging, my wife searched online for books in her native language that might offer practical insight into what we were trying (and often failing) to deal with. Internet trails led to *The Reason I Jump*, written when its author was only thirteen, and produced by a small specialist publisher. Our bookshelves were bending under weighty tomes by autism specialists and autism mem-oirs, and while many of these were worthy, few were of much "hands-on" help with our nonverbal, regularly dis-tressed five-year-old. My wife took a punt on Naoki's book because the author was relatively close in age to our son as well as being nonverbal. When the book arrived she began translating chunks of it out loud at our kitchen table, and many of its very short chapters shed immediate light on our son's issues: why he banged his head on the floor; why there were phases when his clothes seemed unendurably uncom-fortable; why he would be seized by fits of laughter or fury or tears even when nothing obvious had happened to provoke these reactions. Theories I'd read previously by neurotypical authors were speculations that sometimes made sense but sometimes didn't; *The Reason I Jump* offered plausible explanations directly from the alphabet grid of an insider.

Illumination can mortify—I realized how poorly I'd understood my son's autism—but a little mortification never hurt anyone. On YouTube I found a few clips of Naoki and was taken aback at how visibly manifest his autism was—more so than my own son's. This gap between Naoki's appearance and his textual expressiveness made a deep impression. Clearly, he struggled with meltdowns, fixations, physical and verbal tics that not so long ago would have ensured a short bleak life of incarceration. Yet in *The Reason I Jump* the same boy was exhibiting intelligence, creativity, analysis, empathy and an emotional range as wide as my own. What intrigued me as much as anything was that these last two attributes—empathy and emotional range—are precisely what people with autism are famous for lacking. What was going on? The severity of Naoki's autism was documented both in the YouTube clips and in Gerardine Wurzburg's 2010 autism documentary *Wretches and Jabberers*. This left me with two possibilities: either Naoki Higashida is a one-in-a-million person, who has severe nonverbal autism yet is also intellectually *and* emotionally intact; or society at large, and many specialists, are partly or wholly wrong about autism.

Evidence against the "uniqueness possibility" came in the form of other nonverbal writers and bloggers with severe autism such as Carly Fleischmann and (more recently) Ido Kedar and Tito Mukhopadhyay. Naoki's ability to communicate might be rare but it's not one in a million. The "wrong about autism" theory is bolstered by the regrettable errors that could serve as chapter headings in the history of autism. Leo Kanner, the pioneering child psychiatrist who first used the word "autism" in the 1940s in a context distinct from schizophrenia, blamed the condition in part on "refrigerator mothers"—a notion whose public credibility now is on a par with demonic possession, but which maintains some currency in France, South Korea and among an older generation of tenured experts. The 1960s and '70s saw eminent psychiatrists advocating autism "cures" based on electrotherapy, LSD and behavioral change techniques that utilized pain and punishment. I understand that science progresses over the bodies of debunked theories, and I know that judging well-intentioned psychiatrists from the higher ground of hindsight isn't particularly fair, but when I consider the damage they surely inflicted on children like my son, as well as on parents like me and my wife, I don't feel like being particularly fair. The crux of the matter: what if the current mainstream assumption that people with severe autism have matching severe intellectual disabilities is our own decade's big bad wrongness about autism? What if Naoki's conviction—expressed in this present book—that we are mistaking communicative nonfunctionality for cognitive nonfunctionality is on the money?

My wife and I saw no harm in "assuming the best" and acting as if, inside the chaotic swirl of our son's autisms and behaviors, there was a bright and perceptive—if grievously isolated—five-year-old. We stopped assuming that because he'd never uttered a word in his life, he couldn't understand us. We put morsels of food he didn't eat on the edge of his plate of pasta, like Naoki suggests, in case he was feeling experimental that day. Often he wasn't, but sometimes he was, and his food repertoire grew. We started asking our son to pick things up that he'd dropped by taking his hand to the dropped object, instead of thinking *oh, why bother?* and doing it for him. Where possible we gave him choices instead of deciding things for him. We got craftier at discerning his unexpressed wishes rather than assuming his wishes were nonexistent. We began speaking to him normally, rather than sticking to one-word sentences. I didn't know what percentage of these longer, more natural sentences our son understood—I still don't—but I do know that our daily lives got better. I know that day by day and week by week he was more "present" and interactive. His eye contact improved, he engaged with us more, and with help from an inspired and inspiring tutor our son came into the kitchen one day and almost made me fall off my chair by asking, "Can I have orange juice please?" His vocabulary snowballed and episodes of self-harm dwindled away to near zero.

Lacking access to a parallel universe in which I've never heard of Naoki Higashida, I can't know whether these steps and improvements would have come about anyway. We still had, and still have, plenty of less-than-great days. Autism is not a disease, so there are no "cures"—and never give your credit card details to anyone who tells you otherwise. To labor the point: *The Reason I Jump* is not a magic wand. But the book did help us understand both our son's challenges and the world from his point of view more than any other source, and this knowledge helped us help him. Some attitudes and habits inhibit development, while other attitudes and strategies stimulate it, and Naoki's book enabled us to identify the latter and shift a kind of pointer in our lives together from "Negative" to "Positive."

Initially, my wife and I translated *The Reason I Jump* into English for our son's special needs assistants because we thought they would also find its insights helpful. I mentioned the book to my agent and my UK editor, who asked to see our samizdat manuscript. They saw its potential interest to a public growing more tolerant of and curious about neurodiversity. My agent contacted the book's publisher in Japan, and soon my UK, US and Canadian publishers made offers for the English translation rights. Naoki and his family accepted. Helped by a superb BBC Radio 4 serialization and an endorsement in the United States by *The Daily Show's* Jon Stewart—a champion of autism awareness—*The Reason I Jump* entered the bestseller lists on both sides of the Atlantic. A documentary about Naoki and his book's impact—*What You Taught Me About My Son*—was made by the Japanese state broadcaster NHK. It was during the making of this film that I first met Naoki in Tokyo, and saw for myself both the challenges he faces when he communicates and his tenacity in overcoming these challenges. After its first airing, NHK received many hundreds of phone calls and emails from viewers requesting a repeat. After its second airing, more viewers called in for a third, then a fourth, then a fifth time. To date, *The Reason I Jump* has been translated into more than thirty languages. To the best of my knowledge, this makes Naoki Higashida the most widely translated living Japanese author after Haruki Murakami.

I was surprised and pleased by the critical and commercial success of Naoki's book, which matters a whole lot more to the big scheme of things than my own fiction. My involvement in the promotion of *The Reason I Jump,* however, gave me a crash course in the politics of special needs. It is not for the fainthearted. Entrenched opinion is well armed, and its default reaction to new ideas is often hostile. While *The Reason I Jump* enjoyed a positive reception, an accusation was leveled that nobody with "genuine" severe autism could possibly have authored such articulate prose: never mind the YouTube clips showing Naoki authoring this same articulate prose. Therefore, Naoki must have been misdiagnosed and doesn't have autism at all; or he's an impostor at the Asperger's Syndrome end of the spectrum, akin to the character Sheldon Cooper in *The Big Bang Theory;* or his books are written by someone else, possibly his mother. Or me. The *New York Times* reviewer cautioned the translators against "turning what we find into what we want." (The subtext I can't help but see here is, "These desperate parents won't face the fact their son is a vegetable so their objectivity is compromised.") Elsewhere, Naoki has been accused of seeking entry into the guru business. You really cannot win. Of course, Naoki hopes that his writing contributes to a better public understanding of autism, but he is all too aware of the limits imposed by autism upon his knowledge of the neurotypical world. Reading newspapers isn't easy for him and politics can seem baffling. As an ex-pupil of a special needs school he knows that autism comes in many shapes and sizes, so his observations on autism won't be, and can't be, universally applicable. Naoki is nobody's guru: he'll answer questions as best he can, but you take what you need and leave the rest.

My most instructive experience of all was being told point-blank by a fellow contributor to a radio program that *The Reason I Jump* couldn't be genuine because Naoki employs metaphor, and people with severe autism can't understand what a metaphor is, let alone create one. In fact, I've watched Naoki spell out similes and metaphors on his alphabet grid on a number of occasions, but that day I found myself in one of those no-win situations where protestations of probity only persuade your accusers that there's no smoke without fire. My co-contributor's son also had severe autism, and I've tried hard to understand her indignation. To be told that we've been underestimating our child's potential can feel like we're being accused of collaborating in our child's imprisonment, and what loving, self-sacrificing mom or dad would sign up for that? An impulse to shoot the messenger is understandable. As my own prickly response to the *New York Times* review shows, the skin of parents whose kids have special needs is membrane-thin and packed with nerves. However, our compass should surely be the question, "What is best for the well-being and life chances of our sons and daughters?" Ultimately, I believe that while severe nonverbal autism does indeed *look* like a severe cognitive impairment, the truth is it's not: it's a severe sensory-processing and *communicative* impairment. These words hold a world of difference. To deny that a severely autistic brain may house a mind as curious and imaginative as anyone else's is to perpetuate a ruinous falsehood. (The historical analogy is deafness, which from Aristotle's era until the advent of sign language in the nineteenth century was also thought to be indicative of a severe cognitive impairment—hence the synonym for stupid, "dumb.") If a critical mass of people hadn't called time on previous "truths" about autism, the Refrigerator Mother theory—or even the Demonic Possession theory—would still be reigning supreme. Naoki and other nonverbal autism pioneers may be flagging up the next paradigm shift toward a truer understanding of the condition.

Naoki published a number of books in Japan after *The Reason I Jump,* but it was this present volume, *Fall Down 7 Times Get Up 8,* published in 2015, that my wife and I found to be the most illuminating and helpful. A person's autism doesn't conveniently peter out at a certain age, nor does it stop evolving. Our son is now eleven and we've already found this volume to be a useful source of insight into how adolescence can impact upon autism, as well as an indication of what to expect further ahead. Most of its short chapters were written by Naoki for his blog between the ages of eighteen and twenty-two, though he often analyzes his younger self from his more mature perspective. So we hope this new book will be of practical help for other "autism insiders" with both young and older teenagers on their hands. For general readers, we hope the book will offer another opportunity to slip into an autistically wired brain. Its range of topics is more diverse and magpie-like than *The Reason I Jump,* and showcases its author's growth and engagement with the world. If *The Reason I Jump* was a text by a boy who had severe autism but who happened to be able to write, *Fall Down 7 Times Get Up 8* is a book by a writer who happens to have severe autism. Autism is still Naoki's prism and lens, but the chapters add up to a kind of collage-portrait of a young man learning to coexist with a mind and body not always at his beck and call, and carving out a niche for himself in the neurotypical world.

The inclusion of a short story, *A Journey,* inspired by one of Naoki's grandparents' experience of dementia, represents a deeper hollowing-out of this niche. The first-person narrative is powered by a gradual reveal, emotional twists and a dreamlike strangeness, and refutes the received wisdom that people with autism can't emote, feel emotion or see the world from other people's points of view. Nor does it lack metaphors. Also included is an interview (in two parts) from the Japanese edition of *The Big Issue,* a magazine sold by homeless people and the long-term unemployed. Naoki was a regular contributor to the magazine, and the quirkier than usual questions—provided by the magazine's vendors and staff—prompted Naoki to consider some topics he hasn't addressed elsewhere.

The title *Fall Down 7 Times Get Up 8* is borrowed from a Japanese proverb about the merits of persistence, and the book offers experience, advice and hope. Its pages map the limits placed by nonverbal autism upon its author's life, but also describe how Naoki has been able to transcend, re-negotiate or just learn to live with those same limits. The book shows how a disability can be turned into a field of endeavor and the pursuit of a purposeful life. If this is possible for Naoki, it may be possible for others, too.

Autism has a habit of making clean labels like "verbal" and "nonverbal" murky. With neuro-atypical people, communicative ability exists on a spectrum and not in a binary yes/no position. Whenever I'm asked "Is your son verbal or not?" in order to reply fully I have to explain that while his comprehension appears to be good and he can name many hundreds of objects in English and Japanese, his spoken communication is limited to a few phrases, and he's never had a conversation longer than three or four exchanges of these phrases. I cannot know for sure whether he understands none, some or all of a conversation between third parties. If I *could* be sure, it wouldn't be autism we were dealing with (and if I had £10 for every time I've said that last phrase, I could buy a mid-range family car). Autism is a relative thing as well as label-resistant. Compared to some of his peers who have never uttered a word in their lives, and indeed compared to Naoki, my son is rather verbal; but relative to his neurotypical contemporaries, he's a step away from muteness.

The label "nonverbal" as applied to Naoki also requires some explanation. He has a near total inability to conduct a spoken conversation, and a near total inability to give verbal answers to questions. He is better able to deploy the short menu of set phrases drilled into Japanese children and used throughout their lives—an *"itte-kimasu!"* when you leave the house, a *"tadaima!"* when you get home, to cite two of Naoki's examples in this book. Another word he uses is the universal pre-meal expression of gratitude *"itadakimasu,"* though this has morphed into a fixation whereby he has to check that every other diner in the room has also said it. (Problematic at large gatherings.) If Naoki's mother uses her ordinary voice when she calls out his name to check where he is in the house, Naoki is unable to respond. If she uses his full name in the formal manner of a schoolteacher taking the class register, however, Naoki can confirm his presence verbally. He can also say—or, more accurately, is compelled to repeat—words or short phrases that have embedded themselves in his mind. These might be advertising jingles, place-names or words that catch his fancy. Verbal fixations are more deeply rooted: during most of a twenty-minute drive along slowish winding Irish country lanes, Naoki repeated the Japanese word for "expressway" in order to prompt his mother into replying with the sentence "No, it's an ordinary road." (As he explains in one of the chapters here, Naoki would love to stop being a slave to these verbal overrides, but the fixation is insurmountable.) In his book *Ido in Autismland*, Ido Kedar—another "nonverbal autism text-communicator"—memorably notes that resisting a fixation is as difficult as stopping yourself from vomiting. Naoki's verbal comprehension, however, is comparable to a neurotypical adult native Japanese speaker's. In general he understands my less-than-fluent spoken language, but because he's unable to let me know that he has understood I can be left dangling until he begins to spell out his answer letter by letter on his alphabet grid. Naoki's public presentations consist of him reading a prepared text aloud to an audience. This he can manage, with effort, though the strain often heightens the pitch of his voice. If all goes well he can conduct an after-session Q&A, where questions are asked orally and answers given via the alphabet grid. Environmental factors come into play: Naoki seemed to be able to focus on his alphabet better sitting across from me at a desk, while his mind wandered more when sitting on a low sofa for the benefit of a TV camera. One's position on the verbal-nonverbal spectrum can fluctuate according to mood and stress, and shift in the long term. Naoki has only ever answered one of my questions aloud, without using his alphabet grid. We were at lunch. His answer was a simple "Yes" and the whole table smiled in surprise at this achievement, Naoki included. (I'm embarrassed to admit I've forgotten the question.)

Naoki's autism is officially classified as "severe" by the Japanese authorities and he carries an ID card bearing this designation in case a swift explanation is needed. What the designation "severe" involves, however, is as case-specific and relative as the label "nonverbal." My own son is free from many of the classical autistic "tics" that Naoki is burdened with, and over short periods he can even pass as neurotypical. In contrast, ten seconds in Naoki's company is enough for his autism to become unmistakable. My son, however, shows no sign—yet—of being able to communicate the richness of his inner life in the way that Naoki can.

Whose autism is more severe? An accurate answer isn't straightforward. I accept that we need words for degrees of disability, but I've developed allergies to the current terminology of "severe" versus "mild" (redolent of colds and curries) or "high-functioning" versus "low-functioning" (Commander Data from *Star Trek* versus a 1980s home computer). Not long ago I met up with an old acquaintance whom I hadn't seen since my son was diagnosed, who said—with the air of one who doesn't waste time beating around the bush—"So, I understand your son's severely autistic?" Apart from feeling a bit stung, I felt stumped by the paucity of the question. The severity of my son's autism varies wildly from aspect to aspect—communicative, behavioral, self-management, sensory processing, gross and fine motor control. Other variables are mood, tiredness and even the time of year (watch out for November, after the clocks have been turned back an hour). Shorter answers to the question "How autistic is he or she?" are blunt and reductive, yet their ramifications—in education, in the provision of disability allowance—can be life altering.

As I explained all this to my acquaintance, I wished that autistic severity and mildness could be calibrated in terms of ink-cartridge colors, with yellow at the Asperger's end, magenta at the harder-core pole and cyan in the middle, as in: "Well, his autism's functionally fairly cyan, but if people are telling him *No!* all the time it can get splotchy with magenta. Mind you, when he's writing words on his Magna-Doodle or kicking ass at *Temple Run* on his iPad his autism glows canary yellow." That works for me; if it works for you, pass it on.

To conclude: the translators hope that *Fall Down 7 Times Get Up 8* will find a place in the growing corpus of "autism-witness" texts that inform the public, help to dispel myths and misconceptions past their expiration dates, promote the cause of neurodiversity, and encourage people to think twice before using the word "autistic" when they mean "anal" or "uptight." Autism is a fact of our world, which shapes the lives of millions. We cannot change this fact, but we can change our attitudes.

## A NOTE ON THE ENGLISH EDITION

This edition of *Fall Down 7 Times Get Up 8* is supplemented by three chapters from Naoki Higashida's 2013 book *Aru ga mama ni jiheisho desu* and several new chapters written in response to questions from the translators between 2014 and 2016. The author has also revised or expanded a few chapters, and approved the resequencing of the original text into eight thematic sections. The story—*A Journey*—was written in 2015 for inclusion in this edition. The interview from the Japanese edition of *The Big Issue,* a magazine focusing on social issues and sold by homeless people in ten countries, dates from the same year.

PART 1

# THE VIEW
# FROM HERE

# 1

## MOTHER'S DAY 2011

There are children who cannot say "Thanks for everything, Mom." There may be mothers who are saddened by this, and there may be mothers who feel a kind of grief over never receiving a bunch of carnations on Mother's Day. I'll never truly experience the sorrow these mothers are feeling, I'm afraid, but I do know exactly what those children who can't express their gratitude are going through. Mother's Day is supposed to be the time of year when we show our appreciation for everything our mothers, who we love, do for us. In my case, however, I'm unable to utter even a simple "thank you." It's wretched and it's miserable. I'm sure that if a nonverbal person like me could speak fluently all of a sudden, the very first words he or she would utter would be, "Thanks so much for everything, Mom." Please remember: there are young people, like me, who dream of a day in the future when we too can say these few words.

## 2

## "IT'S RAINING!"

A sudden shower arrived out of nowhere. As soon as Mum heard the sound of rain she cried, "It's raining!" and dashed upstairs to the balcony to gather in the washing without looking out of the window. I just watched her, no doubt seeming a bit vacant. What follows is a chronology of what went on inside my head as this scene unfolded:

1) A million pitter-patter-pitter-patter sounds.
2) I wonder, What could that noise be?
3) Mom cries, "It's raining!" Then the noise must be rain.
4) So I look out of the window . . .
5) . . . and watch the rain, mesmerized; yet as I watch now, I hear nothing; it's like a close-up scene of rain in a silent movie.
6) Only now does the sound of the rain start to register.
7) I seek to connect the concept "rain" to its sound; I search for common aspects between all the down-pours in my memory and the rain now hammering down outside.
8) Upon finding common aspects, I feel relief and re-assurance.

9) I wonder, How come it's raining now? It was clear earlier.

10) Up to this point, my mother hadn't crossed my mind. Now she comes downstairs, saying, "That shower was on us all of a sudden, wasn't it?"

11) I recall Mom running to the balcony to save the laundry.

12) How could she realize so quickly that it was raining?

If I couldn't communicate via my alphabet grid, my questions would go unanswered and I'd be sad to my core about how little I understood. As it is, I was able to consult my mother about how she identified the rain by the sound alone. She told me: "Well, because that sound's the sound of rain and when it starts raining, we bring in the washing. The weather forecast was saying it might rain today, remember?" I did recall the weather forecast, although to have done so of my own volition would have been impossible. As I remembered the relevant section of the report, the forecaster's words returned and I understood a little more clearly why the rain appeared from nowhere, which eased my confusion and frustration.

What remains a mystery is how to infer that it's raining purely from the noise. To me, the sound of rain is an abstract. Identifying the voices of my family or the trill of a phone, the barking of dogs or meowing of cats, these are relatively easy. Some sounds, however, take me forever to figure out, like the chirruping of cicadas at the start of summer. I sense that I've heard these sounds before but without further clues their origins remain obscure. Even if I could identify the source of rain-noise, making the jump from the thought *It's raining!* to bringing in the laundry would be virtually out of the question. I'd be too occupied just sitting there, entranced.

Rain is a special case. I have certain memories within which rain has left a lasting impression. When I see rain, bitter incidents I have come to associate with it come back to haunt me. Fun things must have happened on rainy days as well, yet somehow it's only the sad scenes which summon themselves up. I have to put a lot of effort into distinguishing "memory rain" from real rain if I want to avoid triggering bad flashbacks. To do so, my mind tends to give first priority to organizing my memories ahead of thinking about what actions I need to take right at this moment. All these transactions are a part of what I need to factor in as I work toward behaving like a neurotypical person.

## 3

# IMPOSSIBLE THINGS

It was when I was trying to close an umbrella that had been drying out that I ran into trouble. One of its two snap-fasteners wouldn't snap shut. Normally it clicks into place in no time at all, so I felt a surge of annoyance and managed to call out, "Mom, to come!" I asked her to close up the umbrella—but my mother couldn't do it either. She peered at the fastener and said, "Ah, it's gone all rusty—that's why it won't snap shut." Being unable to do what I normally can—even very trivial things—is a big deal for me, in a bad way. So I just handed the umbrella back to Mom—that was my way of asking her to try again. This time she showed me how corroded the little fastener thing was, and said, "See? It's all rusted up. There's no way this umbrella can be closed now." Once upon a time, even with this clear explanation, I might have lost it completely and gone to pieces. By this point, however, I was able to accept the situation and give up on trying to close the umbrella.

None of the above was due to greater patience leading to stronger powers of endurance. Rather, I think that my brain, upon fully grasping the cause of a problem, was able to say to itself, *It's okay, that's impossible to fix, you can move on now.*

On the whole I feel I've always understood the causes of the obstacles I've run up against, but my emotions could still be quite inflammable. It helps me very much that whenever a new issue arises my mother gives short, positive, clear guidance and instructions. People with autism might need more time, but as we grow there are countless things that we can learn how to do, so even if you can't see your efforts bear fruit, please don't quit. Our lives are still ahead of us. Some kinds of success can be won by, and only by, sheer effort and sweat. We all have to bear in mind that adulthood lasts a lot longer than childhood. This is what I've been constantly reminding myself.

# 4

# COLD BATHS

One winter day my mother was surprised to find me shivering with cold after I'd just had a bath. She told me, "You ought to make your bath warmer, you know." The thing is, I really love water, and whenever I get into the bath, I just can't help turning on the cold tap and letting the water run. I don't really notice my body cooling down. When the temperature of the bath is down to roughly that of an indoor swimming pool, my body feels as if it is one with the water itself. I feel like I'm a fish or some aquatic creature who has dwelt in the water for aeons.

Of course, I can't very well stay in the bath forever, however much I might want to. Upon leaving the water I always feel a sense of regret, but because my bath is a fixture in my daily schedule I never get too agitated about it. I'm not even aware of having been cooled down by my cold bath until someone says to me, "Wow, your body's really cold" or "Look, you're shivering!" However often this is pointed out to me, I still seem to end up with a bathtub full of cool water. My hope is that by being told over and over that chilly baths really aren't that great for my body, it will gradually sink in.

Provided that life and limb aren't being threatened, and that I'm not overly bothering people, this approach of *it'll gradually sink in* has a lot to be said for it, I think. Every day is so full of challenges and difficulties that if I was more wound up about fixing my autism-derived behaviors now, life would be unbearable. When I was growing up, my mother couldn't be watching over my each and every move—she, too, has had to develop a "hands-off" mode. This approach might not suit every instance of autism, but it's served us pretty well, so far.

5

# WRINKLES

The other day, when I glanced at myself in the mirror, I froze. Reflected there was a face that was not mine. I kept staring, thinking, *What on earth's that strange face doing in the mirror?* Then I heard my mother laughing. "You look like an old man," she told me, "with those wrinkles on your forehead." I was surprised—without noticing, I'd made my forehead go all scrunched up and, like Mom said, there were now three horizontal furrows across my brow. It was thanks to those three lines that I failed to recognize myself in the mirror. I know I'm not brilliant at distinguishing one face from another, but I never would have believed that I could fail to know my own face just because of a wrinkled forehead. It really sunk in for me then: there's a world of difference between merely seeing a thing and knowing what it is.

# 6

## COOL CLOTHES

I've noticed people often use the words "cool" or "hip" when talking about clothing or fashion. This whole concept of "cool," however, makes no sense to me whatsoever. When I do up all the buttons on my shirt, I'm advised, "Best to leave the top one undone." Or, when I zip my jacket all the way up to my throat, I'm told, "You're supposed to leave it unzipped, you know." It's cooler that way, apparently, but to my way of thinking, buttons and zips are there to be buttoned and zipped up, so it feels strange not to. As for the clothes themselves, as long as they fit me and feel comfortable, that's good enough—I don't really care what impression my outfit makes on other people. Sometimes I admire sports people or celebrities or stars, but I never look at their clothes or style with any envy. Fashion just leaves me cold, I suppose.

As an adult, I know that it's not good to wear grubby or inappropriate clothing, and choosing clothes has become a fraught area—I'm simply not in the habit of thinking about my wardrobe and appearance. When I look in a mirror, I never know what it is exactly that I ought to be checking out. Even if I select one point, focusing my attention on it is already difficult. Aspects of my appearance that need fixing don't leap out at me, and I can't distinguish very well between how things look pre-adjustment and how they appear afterward.

I've compiled a few personal "going out" rituals: change into an outdoors outfit, put on a hat, clean my glasses and put them on too, check my belt, tuck my shirt in and so on. Whenever I'm given fashion or style advice, I do my best to take it on board. But I always think that the daily life of the fashion-conscious, with all its dos and don'ts, must get really exhausting.

## 7

# BAND-AIDS

Whenever I get some kind of a cut or scrape, I want to stick on a Band-Aid without delay. Sometimes I put one on not because I'm actually in pain, but because I want to confirm to myself where the "injury" happened. Also, it brings me reassurance to know that the Band-Aid will flag the cut, scrape, scratch or whatever to other people. Having something on my skin that normally isn't there—in this case, a Band-Aid—feels weird, so usually I take it off quite soon. But when I notice my skin is a little damaged, or when it bothers me, I sometimes put another Band-Aid on so that other people will notice it too. Whenever a zit appears under my nose I put a Band-Aid on that as well, which always makes my family burst out laughing. I don't clock that this is funny until I see my family laugh, but I soon forget all about it, so the next time I have a zit in the same place, I do exactly the same thing. . . .

# 8

## JIGSAWS

Since I left school, I've been enjoying doing digital jigsaw puzzles on my computer. I suspect there are many children with autism who really love jigsaw puzzles. When I do puzzles, I pay more attention to the pieces than to the picture. All the pieces might look similar, but in fact, if you examine them closely, you'll see that each one is minutely different in outline.

I don't begin the puzzle by working on the outside edges. Slotting two pieces together is the fun part for me and rushing to the completion of the puzzle defeats the whole point. I don't take much pleasure from finishing it because that means the slotting together—the good part—is over. Once it's done, I like to flip it over so it's back to front. I love inspecting how the pieces all fit together from the plain reverse side, too.

Then, after admiring the beautiful curved lines for a short time, I demolish the puzzle so it's ready for next time. Simple pleasures are jigsaws.

# "LICKETY-LICK"

When I was really small I couldn't eat a hard candy the way you're supposed to. The moment I popped it into my mouth I just crunched it up into lots of hard little bits. I knew what "munching" meant, but I didn't understand the idea of allowing a candy to dissolve slowly in the corner of your mouth. I remember eating those sweets thinking, *Wow, these things are really hard.* My family must have racked their brains trying to figure out a way to get me to suck sweets instead of crunching them.

Then, one day, as I was biting a hard candy into gravel as usual, Mom told me, "No, it's not crunchy-munchy, Naoki— it's lickety-lick." Back then, if I'm honest, I never normally paid Mum's instructions all that much attention. But this time, her "lickety-lick" was so hilarious that it really banged my funny bone. I just gawked at her, waiting to hear her say it again—but then, from the corner of her mouth, there appeared an uncrunched hard candy. Once again Mom said, "lickety-lick," and showed me the candy that had been in her mouth.

This is how I came to understand the meaning and satisfaction of letting a candy slowly dissolve in your mouth.

## 10

# PORTIONS

In the past, I was unable to divide a plate of food into portions. Even when asked directly, "Divide this into two, will you?" I couldn't grasp the concept. A method only became available to me when I understood that dividing something into two could be achieved by transferring equal quantities of food from a big dish, little by little and in sequence, to two smaller plates. It took me a lot of practice—*a bit for you, a bit for me, another bit for you, another for me,* and so on—before I had my method perfected. But I got there in the end. The final step was to learn to be satisfied when the sizes of the dished-up portions are *roughly* equal in appearance. Now that I've reached this stage, I can serve up food even when more than two people are present. Most neurotypical people would, I guess, pick all this up simply by listening as it was explained or else by observing someone as they divided food into portions. In my case, however, even when I have a picture in my head of the completed task, the sequence of steps I need to take to turn that picture into a reality stays unclear. I might watch somebody doing the job I need to do, but my mind won't quite grasp that I'm free to follow suit. It takes practice, hands-on guidance, small steps and "lightbulb" moments for us people with autism to arrive at our hard-won goals.

# TRAMPOLINES AND SHUTTLECOCKS

I jump up and down a lot, but that doesn't necessarily mean I'm big on trampolining. There was a trampoline at my special needs school, so I went on it from time to time, but I don't think that is connected with my habit of jumping up and down on the ground, or with anything else. Of course, any child who really loves trampolines should feel free to go ahead and jump—I'm just saying that the fixed idea that says *trampolines go with autism* can be wide of the mark.

I'm pretty useless at sports in general, even though "sporty activities" are among my favorite ways of spending time. Playing baseball properly, for example, is out of the question for me, but I still really enjoy throwing and catching a baseball. Likewise with badminton. I can't say I'm any good at it, but just hitting the shuttlecock successfully even once leaves me delighted with myself.

It used to bother me greatly not knowing how long a badminton session was going to last, so we would decide in advance either how many rallies we would play or what time we would stop. Even if we were mid-rally and the badminton session was going well, my need to stop at the agreed time would override what I did or didn't want. But then, one day, perhaps because I hadn't played for ages, I forgot to set a finishing time or a rally limit. After a long while, the person I was playing observed, "Hey, today you're not bothered about fixing a time to stop, are you?" That was the first I knew of it—and I was as surprised as he was. The upshot was, we stopped playing badminton that day only when the shuttlecock fell to bits. Thanks to that session, I gained one more freedom.

# 12

# THE BOTTOM-BITING BUG: O-SHIRI-KAJIRI MUSHI

A number of years ago a song called "O-Shiri-Kajiri Mushi" was super popular. I remember feeling astonished when I first heard it because I thought there really must be bugs like that, which go around biting our butts. Probably there were other kids who were thinking the same. What most people found funny about the bug, I guess, was his comic character, but what tickled me was the combination of the words "bottom," "biting" and "bug." Whichever way I looked at it, the arrangement of words struck me as fresh and unexpected, and each time I heard "O-Shiri-Kajiri Mushi" I'd crack up laughing at how funny it was, while wondering how such a phrase could have been assembled. Once people around me caught on that I liked the song so much, they drew me pictures of the Bottom-biting Bug and bought me Bottom-biting Bug soft toys. However, everyone thought it was strange that I wasn't displaying that much interest in them. Back then, it was harder to make myself understood because I was less able to communicate exactly why certain things fascinated me.

Because my mind tends to go blank whenever I try to speak, I can rarely manage to vocalize the right word for the right situation. Occasionally, however, as I'm struggling to express myself, a noise comes out, like "Ah–ah–ah . . ." When I produce this "Ah–ah–ah" sound, my family now knows what's going on. These are the times when I practice verbalizing the words that I wish to articulate. My mother tells me that before babies learn to speak they go through a similar phase. Because I couldn't even show that I wanted to speak when I was small, you could view this "Ah–ah–ah" as a major breakthrough.

Curiously, now that I stop to think about it, when I'm producing my "Ah–ah–ah" I do it spontaneously, almost without noticing. This differs from those times when I'm echoing back or parroting words or sentence pieces I've just heard, and from those times when I'm using formulaic set phrases. Maybe this isn't too far away from how you neuro-typical people experience the flow of natural conversation?

© NHK/UrumaDelvi

PART 2

# TIME
# AND
# LIFE

# "HANG ON A MOMENT!"

People are forever using the phrase, "Hang on a moment!" In the past, this used to vex me because I never had any idea how long this "moment" was going to last. It varies so widely, depending on the situation. A timer might have come in handy, but then again, I'm prone to getting strongly fixated on things and quite possibly the timer itself would have ended up as another thing to obsess about. These days, however, when I'm told to wait for a little while, I'm able to ask the other person, "Until what time?" If something I'm doing is due to end at 3 P.M., for example, and it overruns, I can manage to propose a short extension by uttering something like, "Until it's five past three." How I would love it if I could breezily ask, "At what time shall we call it a day?" or "How much longer should we go on for, do you think?" but articulating such long sentences is nigh on impossible for me. Referring to a clock-time, however, is generally enough for the people I'm with to catch on that what I mean is, in fact, "How much longer?" and to give me a reply. If we *still* overrun, then I'll follow up with a later time reference, like, "When it's three-fifteen."

This is the method I've devised to keep my head together.

## 14

# ADJUSTMENTS

When an agreed time is altered or a destination is changed at the last minute, I can act as if the sky's falling in. I need time to accommodate my inner state to the change in plan. Nonetheless, it's important to go through with the change. By sticking to the original arrangement purely to avoid the fuss I'll kick up, I'll lose a valuable opportunity to practice adjusting to a revised schedule. Forecasts and plans are all well and good, but I think it's crucial to get used to adapting to the unexpected and unforeseen. Taking these changes on board might require time, but it's time well spent, surely. My autism and its fixations could be why I reject adjustments, and although there might exist an array of strategies to deal with this, only those that a person with autism is capable of adopting will be of any use.

My mother monitors and guides my actions, steadily and tirelessly. It's rare that she blames me or gets depressed about something that I've done due to my autism. Even when I'm really not in good form, she doesn't make a big deal about it. This constant stable attitude of hers is how I'm able to strive to do better tomorrow. I, too, aspire to be better than I am.

# THE DAY AHEAD

I've heard this: "The first thing you do when you get up is to work out what you're going to do with the day." In my case, when I open my eyes my first conscious thought is about whether it's 6 A.M. so I can get up. I look at my watch straightaway and, if it's six, I feel relief. If it's already past six, I need to focus really hard on which of my morning chores will be amenable to shortcuts. After that, I check the day on the calendar. Only special occasions or events are written on the calendar, so if today is blank, I know there's an "approximately average" day ahead. I've grown to be relaxed about the notion of "approximately average" only recently. Maybe this is because I'm less thrown by unusual situations. In the past, I had a much harder time if the order of the day's events got switched or if urgent business cropped up unexpectedly. I didn't mind about the change of plan itself; rather, I was very nervous about how I might react to the new situation. I can't stop myself from worrying about vexing other people or getting pushed beyond my limits into a full-scale meltdown.

I'm really not good at staying still. When I'm obliged to sit in one place for any length of time, I soon want to be up and about. Doing nothing drives me crazy and isn't in the least bit restful; action relaxes me and puts me at my ease. I can't explain why very well. It's instinctual, like a wild animal running over a wide plain. I am connected to neither the past nor the future—my life is enabled only by the present moment.

Having nothing to do in the present moment has the same impact on me as having nothing to do for the rest of eternity would. As long as I'm in motion, I feel as if I could become a valid member of society, like everybody else. That feeling, I think, brings solace. Maybe I'm mistaken, but I don't think I am: by being active and in motion, my heart beats more strongly.

# 16

# TIME MANAGEMENT

Listening to my mother and my sister discussing how they handle time, I've come to understand that there are things they do that I don't. These are, first, deciding by what time a certain job needs to be completed; next, working back to the present time to see what the available time frame is; and then, working on the job to ensure it is done by the target time. These calculations, I imagine, are key to turning plans into reality, but viewing a whole day in terms of subdivisions is a skill I seem to lack. I can assemble a daily schedule for myself, but I find myself unable to master time in the way that neurotypicals do. This inability is hardwired in, I suspect, and can't easily be dispelled by effort, training or practice. For me, once time is compartmentalized its "scenes" are fixed and I'm no longer at liberty to change things around.

Some people might think that scheduling is like slotting in variously sized jigsaw pieces into a rectangular puzzle, but that's not how it works for me. By way of illustration: if I'm out with my special needs helper and I'm told, "To get home by eleven o'clock, we need to leave here by ten," then the next time we go out to the same place I'll recall those times and insert them into that outing's timetable. This doesn't mean I determine the time we need to start our journey home by any reference to the time we've been away: rather, "ten o'clock" becomes the "leaving for home" time, "eleven o'clock" becomes the "arriving at home" time, and these two numbers become engraved in my memory as two dots linked by a line.

If my current activity doesn't finish by the time the next one is due to start, I cancel the second activity or push its starting time back. Time adjustment has become possible for me—provided I have someone to walk me through the changes—so I can handle the schedule changes without getting confused, even with my dot-to-dot memory system. The reason I don't fix my finishing time is that if an activity didn't stop at the appointed moment I would simply end up swapping one "block" with another on the succession of events, scenes and items that make up my timetable. This way, I'm not constantly making arbitrary changes to my schedule.

My brain has this habit of getting lost inside things. Finding the way in is easy, but—like being in a maze—finding your way out again is a lot harder. I want to exit the maze right now, but I'm forced to stay inside it. This applies also to time and schedules. They constrain me. I'd like to live without these constraints as far as possible. Students use school timetables and lots of people rely on daily planners and the like, so it's tempting to jump to the conclusion that schedules must be a good thing for all neuro-atypical people as well—and in the context of school timetables whose items occur unchangingly and within a fixed time frame, I find them useful too. However, a schedule made of mere sequences of events unlabeled with a time is an entirely different entity for me, and not a helpful one. Other people might be able to handle changes to schedules quite easily, but when I have to accommodate myself to a change in a pre-fixed plan, I find it utterly exhausting, while assembling actions in a future itinerary is agony itself! I guess in any context there will be a "majority" way of doing things and a minority who must find an alternative. What's important to consider is how best we can address our deficiencies or uniquenesses and what kind of help would make our lives most manageable.

## 17
## SEASONS

Some people perceive one season giving way to the next gradually, but for me they switch over all of a sudden, within a single day, like the turning of a page in a picture book. I'm not saying that I receive no advance warning at all of an impending change in the season. I sense it's coming from people's apparel, the color of the sky and the way the sun glows; and then, like finding the answer to a question in a quiz, as soon as something symbolizing the incoming season appears, I know the new season has arrived. Nowadays I wait for the "changeover day" with great anticipation. I'm one of those people who get anxious when they don't know what happens next, and turning this anxiety into a pleasure has taken me a very long time.

# 18

# MEMORY SIGNPOSTS

There are people who remember they were doing Action A before they got sidetracked by Action B only when it is pointed out to them. These people seem to have no idea *why* it was they got distracted from their original purpose; they just were. I appear to be different: I never forget what I was doing—a household chore, a leisure activity—before I switched to something else. Neurotypical "forgetters," however, possess a palpable sense of the flow of time and this ordinary absentmindedness doesn't cause major inconvenience in their daily lives. This makes me wonder about memory connectivity, and how yours might differ from mine.

The signposts that cordon off one event from another in my memory are indistinct and lack the clarity and consistency of phrases like "until I go to bed" or "every hour." These "memory events," I would say, exist between the core of a heightened emotional state—triggered by something significant—and my return to the condition I was in previously. I asked my mother about this, and she told me her memories exist as a system of summaries, indexed according to how she acted and what she felt at the time. When it comes to memories from long ago, only single scenes of the original events might remain intact.

Our ways of remembering can vary widely, it seems. It interests me how our behavior in the present can be influenced by memory. A memory can be transformed into a joyful or painful one, purely depending upon how we process or "digest" it.

# RIGHTEOUSNESS

Some bask in the light.
Others mourn in shadow.

What is justice?
What is vice?

It's not easy to decide.
All I know is

humans are absurd
creatures, yet wise.

## 19

# LIFE, THE TEACHER

One of the lessons I'm grateful to have learned as an adult is that life serves up hard times to everyone, not just me. I understood this not by having grown into some super-wise, compassionate being, but simply by experiencing life and observing the reality around me. Many people with disabilities are, I think, kept isolated and insulated from society. Please give those of us with special needs opportunities to learn what's happening in the wider world without deciding on our behalves—by assuming *They won't understand anyway*, or *Well, they don't look that interested*. On the surface, a sheltered life spent on your favorite activities might look like paradise, but I believe that unless you come into contact with some of the hardships other people endure, your own personal development will be impaired. A knowledge of one's blessings is a valuable lesson about life, from life.

## 20

# HOW YOU STRIVE

Who would actually *want* to be sectioned off and receive particular treatment, just because they have special needs? I don't like the thinking behind the sentiment, *Oh, we should make allowances because of his disability.* On the other hand, it is a cold hard fact that a lot of us wouldn't be able to live independently. *People with special needs should be accepted into society along with everyone else.* If this statement was put to me I'd agree with it, wholeheartedly, but then again, when people are exposed to a counternarrative often enough, it's that new version which ends up being accepted as the truth instead.

What I wish to say is this: the value of a person shouldn't be fixed solely by his or her skills and talents—or lack of them. It's *how* you strive to live well that allows others to understand your awesomeness as a human being. This miraculous quality touches people. Via this "how," people consider the sanctity and validity of everyone's life, whether special needs are involved or not.

# 21

## SUCCESS

I never dreamt that *The Reason I Jump* would find the audience it has done. To be honest, I still can't believe it. When I was first asked about the book's international reception in an interview, I replied, "I nearly fell off my chair in shock." I admit I felt happy, but I didn't feel proud of myself or a big sense of achievement. I just mean that it all went so far beyond my expectations. That the book has sold all over the world is an enviable thing, I guess, but at the same time I can't help but feel a little ambivalent about success. I don't view myself as a major literary figure.

That said, what is this thing, "success"? Reaching a goal you set yourself, I suppose. You'll never know if it's paradise or what it is until you attain that goal. Success stays out of reach, sometimes, however hard we chase it. Just because other people acknowledge your success doesn't mean you will derive satisfaction from it. For a person like me with full-on autism, success might be particularly difficult to visualize. In order to succeed you'll definitely have to fail, and for us, old memories of previous failures can be things of terror. For me, success is not some invigorating, emotional experience, like taking in the view from the summit of a high mountain. It's more like walking a high wire, barefoot, in a circus tent. Once you reach the far side you'll earn your round of applause—but the big drop down can happen at any moment! Only people who think of success as an end in itself will see it as a shiny, sparkling state.

Some people with autism can obsess over how not to fail, and I'm not saying it's wrong to be afraid of failure. I'm saying we need to squeeze out every drop of courage and get back up when we do fail. Success can be regarded as a product of countless failures; or as something that comes into view after taking many small steps up a steep slope. People generally judge something to be a success or a failure according to results, but I think there's more to it than this. I'll respect a person who's still at the foot of a mountain but standing firm and looking up at the peak. In the eyes of even those people who seem to be furthest away from "success" you might find reflected the image of a beautiful mountain. I'm truly grateful for my luck that my words have found an audience; and now it's time for a different, taller, mountain.

# AN ALPHABET INTERVIEW

IN *THE BIG ISSUE* BY ITS VENDORS AND STAFF
(APRIL 2015)

### PART I: A TO M

**A:** How do you usually talk with your family? Do you ever argue? If so, what about?

I communicate with my family via my alphabet grid, or by tracing letters onto their palms. Sometimes I can manage to articulate a word that I've had lots of practice at saying, and other times I produce noises "Ah-ah-ah, ah-ah-ah"— like a primitive caveman—to signal my wishes. Matching situations to the right words is extremely difficult for me. There are times when I get confused and lose my cool when I'm at home, but I don't really argue with my family. Opportunities to argue never really come along. People argue when they don't compromise with each other. I think you can't really change other people, so it makes sense to look for an answer that takes your antagonist's personality into account. Perhaps the reason we don't argue at home is that I try to choose the peaceful way out.

**B:** Do you dream? Have you had any good ones lately?

I do dream, yes. Not long ago I dreamt I was walking a puppy in some unfamiliar place. The puppy started running off and I followed, dragged along by the leash I was holding. We arrived at this huge mansion. My mum came out—she looked kind of doglike—and said to the puppy, "Welcome home, Naoki my dear." Then she hugged the puppy and they disappeared inside the mansion. Meanwhile I went off to my kennel in the corner of the garden.

C: What's the first thing you do in the morning? What do you eat for breakfast? Are you a fussy eater?

On weekdays I get up at 6 A.M. and on weekends it's 7 A.M. The rest of my family is still sleeping, so I go and sit on a chair in our living room and do nothing much. I listen to the birds or watch the second hand of the clock and wait as time passes, not thinking of anything in particular. To begin my day this way is a luxury. At 6:30 A.M. I turn my attention to my morning household chores, like starting the washing machine or drying the dishes. For breakfast I eat toast, *miso* soup and bits and pieces. Foods I don't like include sea urchin, salmon roe, *chawan-mushi* savory custard, coffee and alcohol. My favorite food is fried chicken, hamburgers and fries. I can eat quite a lot.

D: We've heard you like going to karaoke studios. Is singing easier for you than speaking? How do you feel when you sing?

I sing all kinds of songs, from nursery rhymes to anime songs to Japanese pop music. While I'm singing, I feel as if I'm the main character in the song. I really love this. Yes, singing is easier than speaking—I guess it's because songs have rhythms. Reading aloud is also difficult for me. The longer a sentence goes on, the more lost I become. I'd like to keep on reading, but I get anxious about intonation and end up reading the same part many times. Or I get irritated that I keep losing my place while "The End" feels a long way off.

E: Do you have any favorite sports? Which baseball team do you support?

Right now, I don't have any favorite sports or a favorite baseball team, I'm afraid. However, I find the rhythmic motions of athletes' bodies as they run beautiful—I can't help but watch. I really don't care who wins and who loses in sports or games.

F: You wrote a poem once about someone you like. Is there a person you're interested in at the moment?

Not really, no. The whole world of love and relationships is full of mysteries. I know nothing about it. Yet.

G: In *The Reason I Jump* you wrote, "My memory isn't a continuous line but a collection of dots." Does this mean that the things you experience every day add more and more dots to a big blank canvas?

I'd say it's more as if experiences become stars in the sky, one by one by one. A blank canvas is two-dimensional, but my memories are arrayed here and there in 3D. Some stars I can reach out and touch, while others are hundreds of millions of light-years away.

H: At what stage do you consider a person to be finally "grown up"?

Maturity, I'd say, is a matter of progressing ever closer to your ideal self. A mountain has various routes to its summit, and sometimes it feels like you're not making progress, but maybe these times are needed to attain your goal. Perhaps you can't even be sure whether you're making progress or not. I tend to ignore what people think about my progress because I can gauge it myself just by seeing how far I've come. If my present situation slid a little, relative to my past, I'd view it as a necessary stage for my future self. "Grown up": a valid pair of words.

I: When life gets unbearable, what should I do?

Please don't assume there's an easy exit. Be still, be calm, and spend today just living, like you did yesterday. People can live okay without confronting their pain. What brought you here isn't your fault. We human beings have to live each day to its fullest and do our best in whatever environment we find ourselves in. There's no need to feel any shame just because your "fullest" and "best" look different from those of others.

J: It's been four years since I began selling *The Big Issue*, and now I'm starting a new life. Thanks to one of your books [sold exclusively by *Big Issue* vendors in Japan], I'm able to support myself. I can't fully express how grateful I am, and I still read the book when things get too much. What do you do when you're depressed?

First off, I'm really pleased to learn that you're able to support yourself. I get depressed usually when I've failed to do something. My failure will remain in my head as a memory—what's done is done. But if I stay depressed, the failure-memory will be worsened by having a Depressed Me in it. I don't want this, so to avoid it I visualize myself getting back on my feet as quickly as possible. If I can turn a memory of me failing into a memory of a victory over adversity, then I can overcome any failure.

K: In one of your books, you write, "While I don't consider that people with disabilities need be thought of as unfortunates, I think ideally we need to evolve our own sense of values." I just can't help envying other people. How can I live without comparing my own situation to that of those around me, and keep my sense of values solid?

It's okay to envy other people, I think. While you're envying, you also feel a pull to improve your situation. We are human, and so comparing ourselves to others makes us depressed. It's okay to feel that too. You don't necessarily need a solid sense of values just to get by. People change, of course. It's best they do. Our new selves emerge from the times and circumstances we're in and the people we meet. We have no choice but to live among other people. All I'd suggest is, while you're comparing yourself to other people, remember your own blessings.

L: Since being present during the final moments of someone close to me, I've started thinking more concretely about preparing myself for the end of my own life. Do you have any thoughts on this topic?

I'm still too young to answer your question, I'm afraid. Living my day-to-day life *and* thinking about the end of it, that's a little too much for me at the moment.

M: What's the best way to be around and assist people with disabilities? Sometimes I wonder if by trying too hard to be fair and equal, we end up being unfair and exacerbating inequality?

I agree this can happen. People can only understand their own pain. Even a genuine desire to help a person with a disability can become a burden or a discouragement for the person on the receiving end. It is important for helpers and therapists to ask themselves, *If I was the person I'm helping . . . ?* It would be useful also if they double-checked that the assistance they're offering is of real relevance to the person with special needs, and not about gratifying their own desire to care. Easier said than done, I know.

PART 3

# SPEECH
# BUBBLES

# 22

# "I'M HOME!" AND "WELCOME BACK!"

"I'm home!" and "Welcome back!": I'm really not good at this fixed call-and-answer exchange. Sometimes I parrot back whichever one was just said or else I just blurt out the wrong one. This is because the two phrases "I'm home" and "Welcome back" come as a set pair. Every time I've called out "I'm home!," I've received a "Welcome back!" without delay, so the phrases have gotten inputted into my memory simultaneously. When I have to act according to preset instructions, I have to sift through similar memories. Like the credits scrolling at the end of a TV program or movie, these memories replay—without audio, which explains why it's so hard to know what to say at these "I'm home!" or "Welcome back!" moments.

Even nowadays, I'm prone to blurting out phrases I used to intone in my special needs school days: formal announcements like "The work session starts now" or "The class is over." I don't utter these phrases because I want to, or because I'm thinking back to my school days. It's very like a replay button that I have no control over. I used to rehearse these phrases countless times, so they became ingrained in my mind. There are other words I say just for the pleasure of saying them. This is the same as wanting to play a favorite piece of music. I'm conscious of my voice at these times, because I can—sometimes—stop when I'm asked to. It's taken me a long, long time to understand myself to the level that I now do. By focusing on topics like these, you can see that some aspects can be improved by practice while others can't. As a general rule, lessons don't tend to stick if I'm shown how to do things on the heels of a telling-off for not doing them correctly. It's really important that we work out for ourselves why we can't master a skill, and what we can then do about it.

## 23

# WORDS I WANT TO SAY

Quite often I murmur words to myself. Many of these words have no meaning, but others are words I use to communicate. It's easy for people to say, "Use expressions like your tools" or "A conversation is like throwing a ball back and forth," but it's so, so much easier said than done. Being nonverbal creates problems and compounds stress, and those of us in this position are, as you'd expect, desperate to find words when something wonderful or sad or awful has happened. There are other times when we wish we could speak that might surprise neurotypical people, I think. People around us—helpers, caregivers, family—would love to know why a person with autism is sobbing their eyes out or behaving so mysteriously. But in my case, at least, I wish more than anything that I could speak to people in my family and ask them, "What's the matter?" if they look gloomy, and, "Are you okay?" Or, when I've caused some ruckus or problems for people, I'd love simply to offer an apology, to give them a simple "I'm sorry."

These words we really want to say look so straightforward. They're not specialized words for providing reasons or for explaining ourselves. It's the more trivial-seeming, commonplace words that we'd love to have at our command.

The first step toward finding a way to interact with people is to want to. Since I've become better able to communicate with others via my alphabet grid, I've been taken aback by how much my words can affect and even move people. Exchanges of thought are, to a large degree, reliant upon this thing called language. Thanks to it, human beings—and we alone—can truly enter and explore the feelings of others. What an extraordinary skill.

# WE'RE LISTENING

We're listening to everyone around us and we hear you, you know. When people are in the company of people with severe autism, they say whatever comes into their heads, unfiltered. It's as if we don't even exist. The explanation, no doubt, is that we don't react visibly to what is being said.

When people try to teach us things, they apply themselves to the job and deploy various strategies, and when they think they've succeeded, they feel good about it. However, why does it so often fail to dawn on them that if we're smart enough to understand their instructions, we might well also be capable of understanding the everyday language that's going on around us all the time? Might it not be the case that the part we have trouble with isn't working out what neurotypical people are saying, but how to respond appropriately after hearing instructions? Have you never thought, "This person couldn't have performed that action unless he or she had understood what I was saying"?

Regrettably, I can't avoid concluding that too often too many people interpret those of us with autism in ways and for reasons that serve their interests first, and ours a distant second.

## 25

# WORDLESSNESS

Back in the days when I had no ways to communicate at all—no writing, pointing on my alphabet grid or verbal expression—I was extremely lonely. People who have never experienced this will go through life never knowing how soul-crushing the condition of wordlessness is. If I tried to describe what it's like to be nonverbal in the World of the Verbal in a single word, I'd choose this one: agony. And yet, this is also true: if we know there is even a single person who understands what it's like for us, that's solace enough to give us hope.

For a long time I was tormented by the question, *How come I'm the only one here who can't talk? Why me?* I often used to dream that I was able to speak. This chapter might make uncomfortable reading for those of you who live and work alongside people with nonverbal autism, but I'd like you to remember: there are lots of us, and this is what we go through.

None of which is to say that people who can't communicate should automatically be relegated to being sorry objects of pity. By living with extreme hardships day in and day out, by constantly challenging and asking questions of themselves, they search for meaning in their own lives and many of them might, eventually, access a mode of fulfillment beyond the reach of neurotypical people. A worthwhile existence lies in playing whatever cards life has dealt you as skillfully as you can.

# 26

# NOT EVERYONE
# WILL UNDERSTAND

My means of communication is not ordinary. I guess a full scientific analysis of how I do what I do would get quite complicated. In my case, since I've learned to touch letters "freehand" on my alphabet grid—without support from my mom—people generally accept that it's my own ideas that I'm expressing. However, among people with special needs who practice a similar mode of communication to mine, some are working with alphabet grids almost in secret. Perhaps the secrecy is to avoid accusations of "cheating," but I dislike the idea of settling for a position that says, *Look, this system of communicating is valid enough for sympathetic insiders—it doesn't matter what everyone else thinks.* This is tantamount to a cop-out by all involved. In my opinion, nobody who's struggling to master a system of nonverbal communication would back this position. Even if they said as much, I suspect they'd be saying it for the benefit of their parents or therapists, rather than because they honestly believed it.

So what has enabled my achievement? To my mind, a big part of it is that my mother never said to me, "Look, it's good enough for the people who want to understand us: never mind about the rest." Whatever the obstacles that might spring up for us wholly or partially nonverbal people with autism, the ultimate goal is to keep honing our skills until we are understood by everyone. Everyone.

When *you* want to tell somebody something, how do you go about it? Before I could express myself at all, I used to believe that just by learning to communicate a little, I'd be able to make myself understood about anything and everything. Not true, it turned out. Although I can get my meaning over to some degree, much of what I really wish to convey is spoken prayer-like, mantra-like, silently, but over and over, in my heart. Words aren't everything, I've come to learn. Please remember: the reality of a nonverbal life is way, way harder than the verbal majority can imagine.

# RUMORS

It's just not nice
when rumors about you
are flying around the place.

Once you know you're being
discussed, you can't go back
to the way you were.

However, knowing the rumors
are out and about need not
have a detrimental

impact. Rumors per se
aren't bad. What matters is
the use you put them to.

# 27

# QUESTIONS AND ANSWERS,
# ANSWERS AND QUESTIONS

One day I was going out and my mom asked, "Do you want gloves? Or don't you want gloves?" I replied "Gloves" straight off, even though, in truth, I didn't want the gloves. Questions can be really tricky for me. In the past, whenever I was asked a "Do you want *x*, or don't you want *x*?"–type question I used to answer "Don't" because latterly heard words stick best to my memory. To ameliorate this, when people ask me a binary question, I ask them to juggle the positive and negative options around, or to write the question down. This helps to a degree and I echo questions back much less than I used to, but it's still difficult for me to answer as quickly as I'd like, or to express my wishes accurately.

Obtaining items just by using words is a pretty amazing thing, to my mind. As long as phrases for making requests are fixed and limited in number, I think it's possible to acquire them. With lots of practice, people like me can learn these "request phrases" as patterns. The results—getting what you asked for—are immediate and visible, so this approach is well worth the effort. *Responding* to questions, however—that's not so straightforward. Why we still can't answer the same question—irrespective of how often we practice—must baffle neurotypical people. The thing is, at least to me, it *isn't* the same question. You focus on the question's "conceptual workings," I guess, but to get a handle on a question, first I have to sift through my memory for scenes where similar questions were asked; then I have to summon up and deploy the words that worked in those "matching scenes" last time around. Of course, in reality not everything about the remembered scene is going to match the current moment, and unless everything about the questioner—clothes, hair, face, as well as identity—corresponds to the old memory, then a new "Q&A memory scene" gets created by the moment we're in. The question's exact wording, timing and tone also come into play. Video segments and TV commercials are easier to view in my head because they never vary, and in formal classes or lesson-like contexts I find it a little easier to access language than in daily life, thanks to the consistency of classroom routines.

Among people who have autism and speech challenges, I think there will always be individuals whose "verbal blocks" come from the same place as mine. They too, I believe, can unlock language by referencing common points between memory scenes and the moment they're in. This might take a great deal of practice, but their family, helpers and teachers mustn't give up on them. The person with special needs will sense that resignation, lose their motivation and stop trying to speak. This can erode even their will to live. Believe me. Communication *is* the person, to a major degree. Please don't be the first to walk away.

# 28

# THOUGHTS ON WORDS

Spoken language is a blue sea. Everyone else is swimming, diving and frolicking freely, while I'm alone, stuck in a tiny boat, swayed from side to side. Rushing toward and around me are waves of sound. Sometimes the swaying is gentle. Sometimes I'm thrown about and I have to grip the boat with all my strength. If I'm thrown overboard I'll drown—a prospect so disturbing, so laden with despair, it can devour me. At other times, however, even if I can't swim in the water, I gaze at the play of light on the surface, delight at being afloat on it, trail my hands and feet in the sea, and dream of jumping in with everyone else. When I'm working on my alphabet grid or my computer, I feel as if someone's cast a magic spell and turned me into a dolphin. I dive down deep—then shoot back up, break the surface and surprise all the swimmers. The process can feel so free, so effortless, that I almost forget I was ever stuck in that boat.

For me, there are two types of sentences. The first type I write for no audience but myself, just for the pleasure of turning my imagined world into words. Because nobody will read this work I write quickly and almost casually, as if I'm solving a simple puzzle. The second type of sentence is written with publication in mind, so I do my best to edit and correct these to make them presentable. I try to ensure that my autism-influenced senses don't take my sentences too far from the reader's experience. Especially with creative writing, I think a writer needs to work with the reader's imagination in each and every sentence. Narcissistic writing causes nausea for the reader. Writing prose that I know will be read feels like discreetly placing a manuscript on a mountaintop and leaving it there. From a good vantage point at the foot of the mountain, I can look back up and watch travelers finding, crying or smiling over the pages I left up there. The mountaintop looks far away, but their voices echo down to where I'm listening.

When I'm communicating using my alphabet grid, sometimes I make corrections. If I'm pointing at a "wrong" letter, I don't vocalize it. Then I restart by pointing at the new letters and spell out the words I really mean. Making a correction isn't easy for me, I must admit. Bringing out my inner self already takes up a great deal of energy, so I try to deploy my alphabet grid only after I've arranged my sentences in my head as best I can. If I express myself with concision and accuracy, I don't need to spend too much time on this. Sentences that aren't too long can be stored in my head. Rather than writing them down first and then needing to edit them, I prefer to store them there for a while. When needed, I take them out of storage to see if any parts are broken or if the style passes muster; then I hone them until they're finished.

There are times when all goes well, when I compose a sentence and stand back just to enjoy it. This sensation is like admiring a tall building I've designed. With luck, the building has no wasteful elements and every detail is noted and works. It blends in with the surrounding scenery and looks as if it was always meant to be here. These are the buildings I aim to construct.

When I'm writing a story, I try to inhabit it by becoming the main character. Passing to and fro between the world of the story and my daily reality, the dreaming boy I once was coexists with the adult I am now. Time loses definition. Translating into words the thoughts and landscapes that appear in my head brings me profound fulfillment. I don't really map out my plots or decide upon a structure too much in advance. As I write, a story's elements kind of settle into place by themselves.

Ideas and emotions exist first, to my mind; words come second, to give form to the ideas and emotions. Certainly, people with an impressive vocabulary can express their ideas more precisely, but these ideas exist independently of the words used to describe them. I wouldn't say that the more words you acquire, the richer your sensibilities. Pleasure, sadness, likes and dislikes—we all feel these, but who can capture every last sensation they ever feel in words alone?

I don't have "favorite words" based on how they sound to my ear. Words are animated by meaning, after all. Sounds in nature—the chirping of crickets or a bush-warbler's song—attract me more than the sound of words. The fact that these creatures don't speak in words as such but send out messages using their whole bodies is a mystery to me, a mystery that human beings cannot duplicate.

## WORDS

People, when wounded by words,
replay those words endlessly

and down they sink
into themselves.

Wise to remember:
words are only words.

No need to swallow, too,
the feelings that encase them.

## 29
# TROUBLE WITH TALKING

The other day, when it was time to say "Thank you very much" to my helper for taking me out and bringing me safely home, the phrase that came out of my mouth was "Have a nice day!" I've been working on these verbal set pieces for ages and ages, but I still can't master such simple exchanges. Talking is troublesome for me. I'd like to work through what was happening in my head when I made the mistake with my helper.

1) I wanted to say the correct thing to my helper. (In my head, "Thank you very much" is stored in the "Everyday Phrases" category.)
2) As soon as I tried to express my thanks, my mind went blank.
3) I floundered, having no idea what I needed to do next.
4) So I looked down, and saw the shoes my helper was wearing as he stood in the small entrance hall of our house . . .
5) . . . which reminded me of seeing my father's shoes there earlier in the day in the very same place.

6) The scene of me saying "Have a nice day!" to Dad flashed into my mind.

7) I remembered that I needed to say something to my helper . . .

8) . . . so I blurted out the phrase that was already in my head: "Have a nice day!"

Can you imagine a life where you're confronted at every turn by this inability to communicate? I never know I'm saying the wrong thing until I hear myself saying it. Instantly I know I've slipped up, but the horse has already bolted and people are pointing out my error, or even laughing about it. Their pity, their resignation, or their sense of *So he doesn't even understand this!* make me miserable. There's nothing I can do but wallow in despondency.

The best reaction to our mistakes will vary from person to person, and according to his or her age, but please remember: for people with autism, the pain of being unable to do what we'd like to is already hard to live with. Pain arising from other people's reactions to our mistakes can break our hearts.

# 30

# WORDS OF GRATITUDE

For people who have restricted speech, it's not easy to express a "thank you." Some neurotypical people might find it a bit puzzling that nonverbal people like me use our alphabet grids so much of the time to broadcast our gratitude. Of course, there are also occasions when I want to highlight problems, but I'm extremely unwilling to use up the precious chances I get to express myself on relatively trivial matters. Try imagining you're a resident in a foreign country where you're wholly ignorant of the language, but a person there is taking excellent care of you. Then, one day, along comes an interpreter who offers you a strictly limited period of time in which he or she will translate anything you wish to say. How would you use that opportunity? Would you really want to spend it mouthing off about the miseries you endure thanks to your feeble grasp of the language? Maybe many topics would spring to mind, but if you're with someone you respect, I think the chances are high that, first and foremost, you'd want to express your appreciation. See what I mean? When time is short, most of us would go for gratitude, especially if we don't know when we'll next get the chance—if ever—to show our thoughts and feelings. "First things first" is king.

These days I'm a person who can tell his family whatever I wish to. Time is my ally. This is a luxury I treasure.

PART 4

# SCHOOL
# YEARS

# SCISSORS AND GLUE

When I was in kindergarten I learned how to use scissors and, when shown where to stick my cut-out shapes, I could glue them on. Completing a "scissors and glue artwork" all on my own, however, was a very tall order: I found it nearly impossible to fix the method in my memory, even as I was being shown it. I really envied all the other kids who could finish their cut-out-and-paste pictures without any help and in no time at all.

These days, provided the art books I'm using are geared to quite young children, I can do these tasks on my own by referring to the diagram that shows how the finished picture is supposed to look. Now, I can't exactly blow my own trumpet about this—the exercises are actually for children aged four to six—but I get a lot of pleasure out of doing the required tasks independently. Once upon a time, it seemed unimaginable that I would ever be able to manage this kind of job. It might have taken me thirteen years to get to this point, but at long last I'm able to tell my deflated, kindergarten self, "Stick at it—you'll get there one day!"

# HAVE YOURSELF A
# "WELL DONE!" STICKER

In the past I was totally useless at paper-craft work, even when I was guided through the process. These days I can do it without any help at all, which pleases me no end. When I've finished a piece, I'm supposed to affix a "Well done!" sticker to it. My first completed paper-craft object was a rabbit, so the sticker I chose had a rabbit on it. The next animal I made was a snail, but as there weren't any snail stickers, I asked my mother which one I should go for. She told me I could choose any sticker I wanted from the wide range on offer. They were a kind of prize or reward, she said; "Just pick the one you like." This threw me into a quandary. Expressing preferences is tied to thoughts and feelings, and because I have difficulties with my thoughts and feelings, it follows that I also had problems when it came to selecting my "Well done!" sticker. So as soon as a panda sticker jumped out at me, I unpeeled it and stuck it onto my snail. Mom approved: "That's the way, Naoki, just choose which-ever sticker takes your fancy." To this day, I bet she's con-vinced I have a special liking for panda stickers. This is a classic example of how easily nonverbal children with au-tism can trigger a sequence of misunderstandings.

So, I cannot choose *a* favorite sticker, nor can I choose

*any* favorite sticker. As soon as I'm told to select one, my mind goes into a whirl, the same way it does when I can't express my thoughts or emotions. Because of this, I end up opting for the first one to catch my eye. This might not be the first one I see, nor the flashiest—it's just the one my eye happens to seize upon—and my own volition doesn't really come into it. What's more, if an observer is looking on, he or she can set up a permanent connection between my choosing a sticker and—for example—pandas simply by declaring, "Aha, so it's *pandas* you like!" and "Good choosing!" From then on, that particular choice becomes ingrained as a kind of default pattern.

I can access this default pattern in the future and re-enact it, so the next time I'm in the sticker-choosing situation, the chances are I'll be picking out the panda again. For me, sticker selection never really was the prize or reward that it is for everybody else. Following the beaten path of the fixed pattern is preferable by far to the stress of not knowing what choice I ought to be making—so, nine times out of ten, I take the easy way out. It's not that I feel sorry for myself. This is how things are. I'd just like it if neurotypical people could understand what's going on with us. That's all.

# 33

## MY FREEDOM

"How come I can't talk?" This was a mystery to me for a long time. When I was a young child, I had no idea what was going on and all I felt was sadness. During my primary school days, I began to think I was a late developer. By the time I got to junior high school, I'd given up on the idea that anything at all could be done for me. I think the reason for this was that there was nobody around me with autism as severe as mine but who was also verbal enough to communicate with me.

Later I became a student at a distance-learning high school and was only required to visit the physical school building on an occasional basis. My life started being different from that of most other people my age. Rather than the viewpoints of other people, what began mattering to me most were the thoughts and ideas inside my own head. There were those who believed that it was vital I carried on going to a regular school every day, like ordinary students, perhaps because young *hikikomori* people begin their permanent withdrawal from society by refusing to go to school and end up never leaving their bedrooms. For me, however, those few years "out of the system" turned out to be invaluable in terms of working out how to live according to my own free will.

Living in a way different from everyone else requires a degree of courage. While it's true that living with your family restricts your independence in some respects, the independence I'm talking about is more to do with the freedom to live as myself and be what I am in the wider society. So now I'm grateful to my family for giving me the space and the freedom I needed.

# 34

# FRIENDLESSNESS

We are taught at school that it's a good thing to make lots of friends. There are some kids, however, who are just no good at it. And because children with autism are poor at interacting with others, many of them have next to no friends, and we can safely assume that some of these get teased or bullied by their peers. The bullies don't mean to cause serious harm; they just throw their weight around because it's fun. Some grown-ups tell the bullied kids simply to put up and shut up, even admonishing the victims and telling them, "Ha, there's worse than that waiting for you out in the big wide world!"

As far as I'm concerned, there's no need whatsoever to "practice being bullied." Acquiring superpowers of endurance is not something children need to be learning before they enter society at large. It is only the person being bullied who understands the true cost of what they suffer. People with no experience of being bullied have no idea how miserable it is to grow up being picked on the whole time.

I would like people to stop pressuring children to make friends. Friendships can't be artificially created. Friends are people whose respect and mutual support occurs naturally, right? Whether or not we have lots of friends, every single one of us is the main protagonist of our own existence. Having no friends is nothing to be ashamed of. Let's all follow and be true to our singular path through life.

# 35

# SCHOOL

During my days at primary school, I used to think I was a miserable, unfortunate case who nobody understood. Only my mom was on my side, and even she was only an ally—an alliance that hardly dispelled the hardship of being in a regular classroom while feeling uniquely different from everyone else. *Why can't I speak? How come* I'm *the only one who can't do it?* How I used to agonize over these questions as I watched the other kids doing all kinds of things effortlessly that I'd never be able to manage, not even if I spent my entire life trying. Every time, I just wanted to break down and cry.

I stuck with my regular primary school until fifth grade—age eleven—but it had become so physically and mentally exhausting by that point that I transferred to a school for children with special needs. My feelings about the move were ambivalent, and remain so. In one sense, it felt like I was running away, and, once there, it took me a whole four years before I found a path to my authentic self. On the other hand, until then I had never observed a class in a special needs context and I was surprised by the big differences between classes there and the education I had been used to. While I was conflicted about the "special needs" label, the kindness I encountered from both teachers and students—unthinkable at my previous school—took the edge off my unhappiness. There, I was no longer a "problem case" but just a regular student. Some students were more capable than me while others had more severe challenges, and for the first time I realized how many neuro-atypical children existed in the world.

The school for children with special needs afforded me the freedom to be what I was, but it became less a place to receive an education and more a place to think about my autism. Time passed without my really doing a great deal. The classes were, in theory, tailored to each student's disability profile, but in practice the teachers had enough on their hands just handling the students' routine requirements. Some students were "long termers" who had been there since first grade, while others, like me, had transferred in from regular schools because it was thought they were better suited to a school designed for special needs. Looking back, most of my classmates seemed to enjoy their days at school without any complaints, but I still wonder if they all believed that this was the place they truly belonged?

That said, my new school was a place where neuro-atypical students were at least free from bullying or ignorant verbal reprimands. The school taught me the importance of being able to accept assistance and of being respected and valued by others. I learned that we all have a right to live as a human being should live, and that happiness is attainable whether we have a disability or not. I saw a future path leading first to a high school for students with special needs (to which my new school was attached) and then to a work center for people with disabilities. I resolved to increase the range of things I could do without assistance, to work at becoming as independent as possible and, to the best of my ability, to avoid inconveniencing others. I thought that any aspirations outside this future were unrealistic because I was now where I belonged. I consigned any memories of my previous primary school to ancient history.

## 36

# BACK TO SCHOOL

There were lots and lots of kids with autism at my new school for children with special needs. I had rarely encountered anyone with autism walking around town; I had been the only one at my local elementary school. But at my new school, you could spot tens of students with autism at a single glance. Retrospectively, I understand now that a belief was ingrained that neuro-atypical children belonged nowhere *but* at schools for children with special needs—end of story. I don't mean that I was especially sad or lonely at my new school. I wasn't. I just mean that there was no questioning of my fate.

I can't really say that I've ever hated the fact of my autism. Perhaps this arises from my never having been *not* neuro-atypical, but I suspect it's truer to say it's because I had a sense of self-esteem that existed independently of my autism. Thanks to this, I guess, I was able to imagine myself going on to study at the high school for students with special needs, and then joining the local work facility for adults with disabilities. Despite this, however, once I finished my junior high school, I took an alternative route. I enrolled in a distance-learning high school and began to aspire to being a writer. Why the change in plan?

I was changing inside. I began to realize that I was allowing a system to make my life decisions for me, and I started questioning things for myself: *Must the fact that I have autism dictate every aspect of my life?* and *What do I want my life to be* for? For whose benefit would I be attending the special needs high school and work center? If it was for my benefit, why was I so ambivalent about the prospect? Or was I just running away from something? I wouldn't deny that I had learned a lot about many subjects at my school and had connected with myself as a person with autism. Equally, I often wondered why being there in the first place felt compulsory. For the first time, I understood that what is appropriate for some people with special needs is not necessarily appropriate for all, or at least not for me.

People with special needs who can't express their opinions never get any say in their education. However hard we work at it, we might never achieve the desired result. What's more, when the special needs education falls short of its targets, the blame is often parceled out to the parents or the child in question. Education is supposed to help the child and parents: it mustn't end up being a kind of holding cell. For this reason, our education must not be overly defined by the views of outsiders, or be unquestioningly compliant with the values and beliefs of specialists. Of paramount importance is that the special needs education be a suitable fit for each and every student.

# 37

# NEW TERM SHYNESS

Two mysteries always jumped out at me when I was attending a mainstream school: first, that on the first day of the second term, all my classmates looked really shy as they arrived at school; and second, that the atmosphere in the class took so long to revert to how it had been before the long summer break. When I asked my mother the reason behind this, she replied, "It's because your classmates haven't seen each other for so long."

While I feel the pleasure of seeing a friend after a long absence, I don't really understand this shyness at all. I've been trying to understand the reasons behind it. Could my classmates have been wondering about whether they and everyone else had changed over the holidays? By taking in each other's faces and by talking, they gradually got their relationships back on the same footing as before. What surprised me—and surprises me still—was, first, how almost all my classmates exhibited that shyness; second, how everybody else accepted the shyness as normal; and third, that the same air of awkwardness occurred after every long break.

I found all this deeply interesting. My guess is that because I'm not so conscious of the flow of time, a holiday of a month is merely one more scene embedded in the past. People who can remember the events of their lives in the correct order, on the other hand, need time to realign their pre-holiday selves with their post-holiday selves.

# 38

# LESSONS IN HINDSIGHT

I look back now at my regular school for neurotypical kids. For sure, there were things I couldn't do on my own, and for sure, this could get depressing and tough. However, I studied and I took part in sports to the best of my abilities at the time, and while the effort eventually overwhelmed me, at least I was there for a while, laughing and crying and losing my temper along with my peer group. My regular school was an important training ground where I could learn about living in society. I regret not understanding this at the time. School doesn't last forever, and sometimes I have misgivings about separating children with special needs from mainstream education completely. Is it too much to ask that the neurotypical majority make a little effort to understand people like me, who tend to remain off their radar? Yes it is, it seems.

I accept it might be impossible to study exactly the same things, but it should be possible to share school buildings and grounds. At my regular school I learned about human rights and social cohesion, but when it came to my education, these principles didn't seem to be applied. People with special needs don't just require practice at the things they can't do. They also need—crucially—to look for meaning in their lives. I wish more people understood that there are individuals who lead mostly invisible lives as they cope with disabilities and challenges, and that to observe them doing so is to reflect upon one's own life. This is not to say that people with autism want you to think, *Oh, those poor things!* or *I'm so sorry for them!* All we want is to live alongside everyone else. People getting on with life and working hard together is a wonderful thing. Yes, the neurotypical majority might be more productive than us, but we, too, want to embrace life and be of use to others as best we can. Must people born with special needs lead unseen lives, as if we're hiding ourselves away? Unfortunately, we are too often kept apart from society at large against our will. This denies us the chance of a meaningful life.

I'm not here to make demands for improvements in the daily condition of people with special needs. I appreciate that neurotypical people have busy, stressed-out lives and that it's thanks to you that we can lead tolerable lives, at least. But surely there's a lot we can learn just by being together, by considering how you see us and how we see you? The way we live our individual lives feeds into society's sense of values. There is more to mutual aid than material exchange and physical support. There is more to human life than eating and sleeping.

The reason I didn't attend the high school section of my special needs school was that I wanted to choose my own future. Just like anyone else would. Naturally, this choice entailed certain responsibilities, and the reality my decision led me to wasn't always a bed of roses. But it was *my* choice, and my first step toward my vocation. Working at a facility for people with disabilities is in no way a negative thing—everyone's life is valid—but fencing us off from society does us no favors.

I can't know everything there is to know, but I think that how we choose to navigate our lives should be an individual choice. The notion that we are best off living in isolation should not be taken as a diktat. It is by observing other people's lives that one comes to an understanding of what is right for one's own life.

There are many ways of living, and this goes for people with special needs as well. We grow and bloom best in company. There must be so many of us with dreams that we yearn to see come true someday. May your futures and our futures come together.

## PROCESS

Some people say
results aren't everything:
process matters more.

Could this be because,
as you strive goalward,
it's your inner state,

not the actions you take,
that count? Belief in oneself
can win the day.

39

# WORDS OF PRAISE

Praise is not a fast track to self-acceptance, I believe. Praise derives from the judgments of others. It is distinct from whether an action truly went well or not. It is separate from how we think and feel inside ourselves. Many people seem to buy into a belief that praise boosts our will to succeed and nourishes our confidence, but I'm not so sure if that's always the case. Of course, little children love being praised and it's always pleasant to receive a compliment from an impartial observer. When I was a student at my special needs school, however, I used to have mixed feelings about teachers who would heap exaggerated words of praise on students for quite trifling achievements. There were children from all across the spectrum at my school, so sometimes it might have been appropriate, but the teachers would apply the same strategy even to much higher-functioning students than me. It was the same story with our parents or guardians—we got praised for the tiniest matters, or for things we had mastered ages before. Everyone was so unfailingly nice to us, it was as if every mean person had been erased from the world. Gradually, the atmosphere wore me out. It really felt like I was trapped in a school for infants.

My gratitude to the teachers at my special needs school is profound, and I'm conscious of how diligently they cared for us pupils. Being praised isn't a hostile act, but it's worth considering whether the person with autism wants the praise as much as the praisers assume they must. Children with special needs already know they're different, and they all live with hardships whose full nature only they can understand. Teachers and adults tend to focus on finding things to compliment. Compliments can help us to feel cherished and encourage us to focus on what we're good at. However, whenever I was praised for doing something that, by rights, only a young child should be praised for, I felt as if my future was deferred indefinitely, yet again.

What I, as a person with special needs, longed for was to be taught what role, what purpose, I could have in society, and how to attain a level of independence. Some people might think, *No no, these questions are too taxing for children to understand*. The answers, when put into words, might appear to be too complex for us, but I'd argue that that's only because we are often so poor at handling language. I'd argue that every neuro-atypical person is thinking the same way about a life with meaning and independence. Children with disabilities might, to your eyes, look stuck in a perpetual childhood, but our thoughts and sensibilities evolve constantly. So, using vocabulary the child understands, please show them how they can live their lives to the full.

## 40

# THE WAY YOU ARE

Many people long for others to accept them the way they are—especially, I suspect, people who know they'll find that acceptance. But for those of us with disabilities, what does "the way you are" even mean, exactly? When a person who lives with constant challenges is told, "Don't worry, you can carry on being exactly the way you are," I sometimes wonder if that person actually *wants* to carry on in that same mode. The phrase "The way you are is fine" contains kind sentiments from the person saying it, I know; and I know the speaker believes the phrase will put the person it is being said to at ease. What I'd like to query, I guess, isn't the phrase itself, but the subtext underlying it. If the speaker means, *You know, you're already good enough just being the way you are,* then some people will be delighted to hear it, but I suspect others will be thinking, *No thank you very much: I don't* want *to be stuck the way I am now for the whole of the rest of my life.* In a way, it's easy enough to accept a person as being the way they are. What matters long term is what follows on the heels of the assurance, "It's okay, just be the way you are." That's the kicker.

# 41

# ADVICE TO MY
# YOUNGER SELF

If I could speak to my thirteen-year-old self, I wouldn't offer bland words of easy encouragement. Just being told, "Do your best!" and "It'll be all right in the end" wouldn't have meant a whole lot to me back then—life was simply too much of a struggle. No one has an objective view of the good and bad aspects of their present selves, I believe: it's only via hindsight that we understand what we were think-ing. Positive words uplift people, I know, but I'd prefer to impress upon my younger self that life is short. People keen to embrace tomorrow are people imbued with hope. Once we grow to understand that our lives don't—as we once imagined—go on forever, we can roll up our sleeves and get on with things.

I was thirteen before I fully accepted the fact of my dis-ability. Prior to then, when I was still a child and thinking of not a lot apart from myself, I couldn't begin to visualize my future. Time's passage and flow seemed unending, like being on a swing that I never got off. So I'd like to tell my thirteen-year-old self that the swing will one day stop and that, until it does, by swinging with all your might, the same old scenery will evolve. Once you've felt the presence of death, you know the brevity of life. Life is short. Life is a sequence of regrets. But all the worries troubling you now will soon recede, into the past.

The final thing I'd like to tell my thirteen-year-old self is to consider for whom he is living. I'd say, "Please live your life for yourself." Parents, teachers and caregivers continue to look after us, and of course we mustn't forget to thank them. However, our lives are our own lives. We should live for ourselves with pride and with our heads held high. In the past, I used to despise myself for being so useless—but the one making that judgment was also me. I'd tell myself, "Make your life shine with the purity of a flower and with the shimmering of stars. Around you are people who are proud of you and wish you well. In your future are days when you can look forward to your tomorrows."

# A JOURNEY

I took the street I always take, so how did I lose my way? Too weird for words. *Just a slip of my mind, perhaps?* Looking around, that's what I figured. "This place could be any- where": a perfect phrase for this town. I'm supposed to know what's going on, but even where I was standing looked unfamiliar. Looking behind me, I saw a river across the road and, as if my feet had made the decision for me, I began running. Lights were dancing on the river. Here and there were whirlpools in the current. I noticed a person on the far bank staring straight at me. "HALLLOOOOOOOOO!" My voice came out loud, unbelievably loud. Still watching me, the person gave a slight bow and I felt a little reassured. *Well, let's cross over this river and see what's what on the far side,* I thought, and off I jogged. *There must be a bridge around here somewhere.* But I couldn't find one. I was pant- ing for breath now, so I took in my surroundings once again and noticed that the person who had been across the river was now over on my side, so I dashed back the way I'd come. "Excuse me," I said.

"What's the matter?"

I wasn't sure how best to explain things. "Well, I'm kind

of lost." My forehead was all sweaty. "Where is this place? You see, I—"

"Cheer up, you'll be back home soon enough," said the man.

These kind words consoled me and left me embarrassed that I'd been so flustered. *Of course, yes, my family must be wondering where I am.* With that thought, it came to me who this man was.

My father. "Dad," I murmured, and he looked a little taken aback. He was probably thinking, *So at last he's realized who I am.* He clasped my hand and I apologized in silence: *Sorry I didn't recognize you straightaway.* My father and I set off side by side, like we did when I was a kid, and everything was just fine. *A minute ago it all felt like the end of the world—unbelievable!* "Thanks for coming out to get me," I told him.

Dad pretended not to hear me. I wondered why.


We came upon an avenue of gingko trees I had walked down before. Yes, the scene was quite familiar, but I was no longer at ease—I felt as if I was, in fact, in a strange country. Loneliness ebbed over me, so I spoke up again. "Dad, how long will it take to get back?"

My father turned to me. "By the time the sun goes down, I'd say."

"Good," I replied. And for the first time in a long while we spoke about dozens of things—school, friends, the cat, you name it. He took it all in, sometimes smiling, sometimes nodding, sometimes making agreeing noises. I described every last memory I had in my head.

The evening star was out and everywhere around me was tinged with all the colors of sunset. I gazed yearningly at the scene. "What—a—picture . . ."

A silence fell. There was nothing left to tell my father. I was on the point of saying, "Your turn, Dad," but as I looked up at his face, a shadow passed over it. He looked despondent, and I became all flustered: *I have to keep talking about my life, he wants to hear more.* I struggled to come up with more recollections that I might have squirreled away somewhere, but my body wouldn't stop trembling with anxiety. *I've forgotten something, something crucial . . . and now Dad'll be furious with me.*

The next moment, I found myself running off again until, some time later, I finally ran out of breath. *I should be in the clear by now.* I felt like I'd done something bad, but also as though I was safe. Darkness had swallowed everything around me, so there was nothing I could do—I'd have to lie down and go to sleep right where I was.

It was early morning when I woke up. Light bathed my whole body. I felt good, and sang to myself a song I once loved a long time ago. Inches away and everywhere were swaths of wildflowers, all pretty pinks and yellows. A cabbage-white butterfly crossed my vision. *I'm going to catch you,* I thought, and chased after the butterfly: the butterfly fluttered and fluttered and fluttered and fluttered and time and time again I snatched at the thin air, before finally tripping over and landing on my backside. Defeated, I squatted on my heels and raised my head. *Who's that?*

There, in my line of vision, was an old man. His gaze wasn't piercing, but he unsettled me. He was peering at my innermost self, I felt.

I hurried away, trying not to look back in his direction, until he was safely out of sight. Who on earth could he have been? Why was he staring at me like that?

Now that I thought about it, it struck me that I'd probably seen that very same old man yesterday, as well. And perhaps I saw him the day before, as well . . .

*Who knows?* I told myself not to worry too much about it.

I took a nice deep breath, and let it all out . . .

*There's nothing especially out of the ordinary.*

As a mood-changer, I tried summoning up a cheerful memory. Nothing came to mind. *Tired. I must be tired.* A good long rest at home, that's what I needed. So off I set once more. On sunny days, the trees and plants and wildflowers are aglow with life. When I was a child, I used to run around and play in these meadows, catching insects and playing hide and seek. Those were the days. One after another, the faces of my friends visited my mind.

*How is the old gang doing these days?* I wondered.

The greenness around me, meanwhile, was denser, darker and deeper. The life force of nature that envelops this world left me lost for words, and feeling like *I* was the one being breathed in by something, I kept walking. The thought struck me that up ahead lay whatever it was I was searching for.

All of a sudden, as if emerging from a labyrinth, I came upon an empty field and I sat down, sighing. Yes, the scenery here was familiar. I used to be such a cheerful person. I counted my blessings, and smiled . . . but just as I was about to get going again, I heard voices in conversation. *Wow*, I thought, *even in a place as empty as this, there are people*. I got to my feet as some friendly-looking women approached. They wore aprons and shared some tea and snacks with me.

"What a glorious day!" they said. "We're going for a walk. Why don't you come with us?"

"Well," I responded, "okay then."

We set off. Everyone was in good spirits, and kind.

After a while, this white building came into view. One by one, the women went inside. "Why don't you come in?" they asked me.

*Well, why not?* An invitation's an invitation.

But upon reflection, I changed my mind. "I'm sorry," I said, "but I've got a few things I need to take care of—I'll have to excuse myself." Saying this, I bowed.

The ladies objected, "Oh, but you've already made it this far!"

No. My mind was made up. I said my goodbyes and walked away in the opposite direction. Despite what I'd just told them, the people stayed in my thoughts and, secretly, I crouched down in the cover of a large tree growing next to the house. The sound of their footfalls faded away, and by and by the door was locked. I waited a while longer.

Nobody left the building.

*This is not a place where I belong.*

*I can't just stay here indefinitely.*
*No, I have to do something.*
*It'll all work out in the end.*


*Where on earth did you spring from?*

A small girl was at my side. I hadn't noticed her before.

She asked me, "Where are you going?"

"Uh—thataway," I replied, and began walking.

*Yes, that's true—I was going in that direction.*

But after only a few steps I stumbled, tripped over a small rock and smacked my forehead on the ground, giving myself quite a nasty injury. As I was curled up there, the girl peered at my face in concern. "Come on," she said. "I'll help you the rest of the way." I held the girl's hand and she led us away.

*What a helpful child this is,* I thought, *to take such pains over a person like me. I'm truly grateful. I wonder if she's some kind of angel?* So I thanked her.

Step by step by step, on we went.

"Well, we're here," she told me. "We've reached Thataway."

Oh. *We're here already.* Promptly I said, "Now this way."

"Okay," said the girl. She took my hand again and led me away in a new direction. Step by step by step. Her hand was small and gentle, and as long as I was with her, I felt encouraged and that everything was going to be okay.

"Here we are," she announced. "We've arrived at Thisaway."

*I don't want to say goodbye to this girl.* And after thinking this thought, I fell silent, but the girl said, "Don't you understand what I'm saying?" Her eyes filled with tears.

So I grew sad too. I put my hands on her shoulders. "No, I'm sorry, I'm sorry, I do understand." *How awful of me, to make such a sweet little thing burst into tears . . .* This was all too much to bear. I looked up at the great beyond, and bit by bit by bit, my emotions calmed themselves. In every direction, the blue sky stretched away. White clouds floated. *If I was a bird, I'd fly off to eternity . . .*

. . . and my body felt lighter than air, then was lifted up. I stretched out my arms, as far as they'd go.

*Wonderful . . . just wonderful.*

My mind and body felt so free, I forgot I was a person.

"Enough already," I told myself. "That's enough now."

*But what does "enough" even mean, exactly?*

Somebody gave my back a shove, and at the speed of thought I returned to myself. The person who had pushed me was an old man, sturdily put together, who looked at me sternly. We'd never met. I pulled away, or tried to, but he prevented me. When he saw the blood on my face from my wounded forehead, his features showed distaste. I said, "Uh . . ." and placed my hand over my brow.

The old man said, "Leave that alone and come with me" and grabbed my wrist. "Hey," I protested, "that hurts!" But he didn't let go. He strode off, dragging me along after him, until we reached a small room which he pushed me inside. The room held one bed and one chair, and that was it. *Where am I now, and what's going to happen to me?* I began crying and found I couldn't stop. *That horrible old man's the lowest of the low to lock me up and leave me in a place like this! It's not as if I've even done anything wrong . . .*

This was the End—and I was petrified.

"Get me out of here! Help me! Someone!"

I peered through the one tiny window.

The sun was slowly, slowly sinking.

*Ah . . .*

A sunset to darken my heart.


I hadn't noticed that I'd fallen asleep. The curtains were drawn and I couldn't tell if it was night or day. Quietly, I opened the door of the room. The passageway outside was deserted—now might be my chance to make a break for it. As I set foot in the passage, however, the old man stormed up with a face like thunder and demanded, "And where do *you* think you're going?"

*Damn,* I thought. *Now I'm in for it.*

Hoping to avoid trouble, I just put on a pleasant face.

The old man shouted, "What are you doing out at this time?"

Startled by the volume, I scuttled back into my room.

*How* dare *he talk to me in that tone of voice?*

I grew angry. *Well, to hell with him. I'm not doing what he says any more.* That night I was in too much of a state to sleep, but the following day the old man entered my room and gave me a polite "Good morning." I ignored him, which might have annoyed him. He didn't give me any breakfast. I wasn't madly hungry, but when no lunch came either, I said "to myself," in a deliberately loud voice, "My my, I haven't had a single bite to eat." Begrudgingly, he made me a couple of big rice-balls—and after I'd wolfed them both down, the old man hoiked up his eyebrows into an expression of jokey surprise.

Thanks to that funny expression of his, every now and then I'd ask the old man to make more rice-balls. He rubbed antiseptic into the wound on my forehead, put on a Band-Aid and gently smoothed away the pain. *Huh, maybe he isn't quite such an ogre after all.*

All the songs of the birds echoed in the mountains.


One day, I summoned up my courage and told the old man, "You know, I'd like to go home now." He glanced at me but ignored what I'd said, acting like he hadn't even heard. *Who does he think he* is? *How can I trust him a moment longer?* My patience was all worn away, and I snapped: "I want out of here! Why won't you let me go home?" I boiled over and I pounded the old man in the chest over and over. "You!" I shouted, "You! Just *get out* of my sight!"

The old man's shoulders trembled—and then *he* lost the plot. "That's enough already!"

*. . . Am I to blame for being here?*

Am I in the wrong?

*Don't stare at me like that.*

My last hope of ever going home was gone.

I might as well kill myself now.

I can't take any more of this.

Yet my life with the old man somehow carried on. He tried to speak with me sometimes, but I was too grumpy, too sunk in despair to respond. Despite my bad temper, he carried on the conversation on his own. *I wonder if the old man feels lonely?* What passed through his mind was a mystery. From time to time, other people came into my room to clean or to tidy up, but the old man always stayed. Toward these others, he was deferential to the point of subservience, but he always lorded it over me. I disliked the old man for this, for sure, but as I observed him, I began to wonder if he also hadn't been imprisoned here somehow and was being forced into working here against his will. The old man kept expressing his thanks to other people. Up to a point, I even began pitying him, and started treating him a little more kindly. Only yesterday I told him, "This job of yours is really pretty tough, isn't it?" and for the first time the old man gave me a smile. *Aha, then I'm right*, I thought. *Where's the harm in helping him out a little?* So when the old man told me, "Lift up your arms," I lifted up my arms. Or if he told me, "Eat this up now," I'd eat it up for him. Tasks like those, even I could manage. *Someday, I want to get out of here and be free again.* I needed someone to understand that I dreamt about being free again. Some of the weight was lifted from my shoulders by thinking of the old man as a kind of ally. The kind who fortifies you.

Now and then, when the old man wasn't busy working, he would take me outside. Outside the building, the air was fresh and clean. The old man and I sat next to each other on a bench in the soft breeze. I would stare at the ground as he pointed into the distance and said, "Look at that, over there . . ." To be honest, I couldn't make out what he was pointing at, but I'd respond with a "Right, yes . . ." and a nod. I guessed the old man was trying to lift my spirits and give me renewed hope in the future. I appreciated the gesture. Maybe he and I were becoming friends, after all.

Possibly because I was feeling more at home and settled now, I was sleeping better and more often. However long I slept, no one ever disturbed my rest. I'd have this strange dream occasionally. There would be this one joyful Me—full of the joys of spring—alongside another Me, who was sobbing his eyes out. These two versions of myself were unaware of each other's existence . . . as if two worlds were housed in a single ongoing story. There was an assumption that the Joyful Me would get the happy ending, but in fact, both the Joyful Me and the Miserable Me would wind up pretty much the same. I didn't understand why. Surprisingly I found myself sympathizing more with my happier self—after all, the dream Me who had the most in common with the real Me was the unhappier one.

As I lay drowsing, the old man would sing lullabies and gently pat my back. It was embarrassing to be treated like a baby, but as my face untwisted itself and relaxed, the old man watched me contentedly. He took care of me in other ways too. He changed my clothes, he fed me. When had he become so kind, I wondered? We'd talk about this and about that and time passed quite pleasantly. One day, the old man asked, "Are you feeling all right?" and I nodded a yes, but my body felt heavy and dull and once again sleep dragged me under.

The old man who, until recently, had been surly and blunt and angry with me all the time, was now cracking jokes and trying to get me to smile. When he was a kid, the old man must have been quite an expert at making paper airplanes. He made one for me, too. "Hey—watch this . . ." and as I watched, the paper airplane glided by. I followed it with my unblinking gaze. The old man threw the plane over and over again, and when we were finally finished, he placed it in my hands. I glimpsed the shadow of a child and heard a boyish "Yay!" and a murkiness clouded my head. The old man turned away and the door shut behind him. *Thunk.*

Around midnight, I was shaken awake. The old man was there again, tears welling up in his eyes. I stared back at him, astonished. He buried his face in mine. *Why so sad, you poor old thing? There there now, I'm here, I'll take care of you.* Love and only love makes whole the hearts of those made desperate by loneliness. You see, I understand this better than anyone. The old man clasped my hands. They were warm. I couldn't help but feel that I had held these hands a long time ago. *That's right, you did, that's right.* My sense of self closed down and I sank into a place of perfect darkness, far beyond the reach of others. There we stayed until the end of the night. The old man never once left my side.

Without warning, I was seized by severe pain, all over my body. I could hardly breathe. *What do I do?* I looked to the old man for help. He held me and wept. My cheeks were damp with the old man's tears, tears like cold rain. My eyes focused on his face, and *now* came the moment . . . My brain—long since stopped—began powering up again; and my memory—so muddy for so long—now reactivated. *Zap.* Yes, it all made sense, and as everything came back to me, I understood who the old man was. *He* isn't the old man. Not by a long shot! I have it now. This person is . . .

This person is . . .

My son. Crying, like he can't keep a lid on the surge of what he's feeling. My own heart was thumping. *Why didn't I recognize him until now?* I felt wistfulness, I felt acute pain, I felt gouged out. My son's mouth was opening and closing. He was saying something to me, but his words didn't reach me, my ears didn't hear. I placed my trembling hand on the crown of my son's head.

My own son. Crying.


It was all a journey through memory, you see.

It was all a journey made of memories.

A journey of memory.

○ ○ ○

I couldn't believe I'd forgotten my own father was dead, even though he passed away so very long ago. *I'm sorry,* I tried to tell my son, but the words wouldn't come out. I wanted to say them, but they wouldn't come. I heard a rustling sound and a girl was at my bedside. She patted my hand. My hand was wrinkled, like a withered branch. It came to me now that the young girl I had met before was my own dear granddaughter. Gathered in the room were also the caregivers who had been looking after me. One or two were dabbing the corners of their eyes with their work aprons. Others were cupping their mouths with their hands, like they understood I was ready to depart, but were uncertain what to do next. My breathing grew staccato. My jaw thrust up and out. The sound of a death rattle. My eyes welled up, my tears mingling with my son's. My consciousness was fading away. "Dad? Dad!" My son's voice was unearthly. *Don't go!*

By and by, my eyes looked upon nothing.

Upon a world devoid of anyone.

*Am I all there is now?*

Thinking back, I thanked my son with all my heart for caring for me and tending to my needs. From out of the distance, a person in gold slowly approached. She was beautiful. My wife, who died several years ago. I followed her along a path of light, resolving to let what would be, be, and to follow the path to wherever it led.

Up ahead, utter darkness spread and grew.

There was no turning back, but still I hesitated.
A pale hand reached toward me.
Straightaway, I knew whose it was.
*Mom* . . .
I raise both my arms.
I'm lifted.
Up floats my body.
This is the end of my journey.

PART 5

# INNER
# WEATHER

# ONE ARMY FIGHTING HARD

There are times when I wonder where this disability called "autism" comes from. Could it have been created, I wonder, by humankind itself? I can't help but feel that some imbalance in this world first caused neuro-atypical people to be needed and then brought into being. This isn't to say that all of us are delighted to be the way we are all the time, of course. But I refuse to accept it when people view us as incomplete or partial human beings; I prefer to believe that people with autism are every bit as whole as anyone else. We might be different from the majority in diverse ways, but why are these differences negative things?

Just as everyone has a heart, so everyone with autism possesses an array of feelings: real, if invisible feelings. Even among people who can speak, shyness or unwillingness aren't the only reasons why some don't reveal everything about themselves. To display your emotions is, after all, to put your whole self up for scrutiny. Perhaps total exposure of the self is not even possible. Emotions can be unfathomable things—and therefore hidden, even to the self. Yet emotions—as everyone surely knows—are also what make us human.

# EMPATHY AND ENDURANCE

It is often said that we people with autism lack empathy and any understanding of other people's emotions. In my view, however, people with neurotypical brains aren't so fantastic at getting to grips with *our* emotions, either. Anyway, there are times when I can't help but wonder if not being able to divine the inner feelings of the people around us is, in reality, the debilitating problem it's cracked up to be. Shouldn't how we feel inside of ourselves be at least as important? How much use can we really be for other people unless we *first* find the headspace for questions about ourselves—*What are my priorities now?* or *How was I feeling when such-and-such a thing happened?* or *Am I on the right path through life?*—and the answers. Some people with autism might not yet be fully able to understand themselves. Some might not understand others. Some might not wish to *try* to understand. Sometimes a situation occurs when I lose my capacity for patience, even though I fully understand why the situation has come about. Some onlookers might tell me, "You're not patient enough—just show a little endurance!" But how can degrees of patience be measured, exactly? Mastering emotions can be so overwhelmingly taxing that I sometimes wonder, *Am I wholly to blame if I can't handle this?* Our world would improve if the neurotypical majority could try to empathize a little better and a little more often with people like me who "lack endurance."

# 44

# LONELINESS AND AUTISM

The word for "autism" in Japanese—*jiheisho*—conveys an image of people locking themselves up inside themselves. This is misleading. People with autism aren't good at interacting with others, for sure, but our hearts and minds are always open and ready to receive. If we were truly clammed shut inside ourselves, we wouldn't be coming out with our weird utterances or be prone to panic attacks. I take these phenomena as proof that our emotions exist and are trying to exhibit themselves. Some people might not care either way whether the emotions of people with autism are locked away or not, but indifference doesn't help us. The neurotypical public needs to know that the failure of people with autism to communicate doesn't stem from inner self-imprisonment: it stems from a failure of others to see that we are open and receptive. To venture out into the world requires help from other people. Please lend us that support as we strive to live in society.

I always think of the loneliness of nonverbal people with autism as being like the darkness before the dawn. Hope might be just around the corner, but we can't imagine that the night will ever end. In general, people just don't understand how lonely nonverbal people with autism can be. When I stop and think about it, I see that everyone is kind of alone from the day they're born until the moment they die. People with whom we can share *all* our days and thoughts don't actually exist. It's to nullify this essential loneliness that people connect with others, I think . . . Meaning that nonverbal people with autism, who can't make these connections, are probably the loneliest souls of all.

Looking at it another way, however, if we accept the idea that human beings exist in isolation, then we nonverbal people with autism really aren't so unique. Memories remain, equally and evenly, whether you're a solitary person or not. The heart treasures the memory of giving and receiving love, whether you can connect with others via language or not. Maybe we'll only discover whether our lives were truly lonely when we're on our deathbeds.

Some of you might be concerned that people with autism have nobody to share their feelings with. Because we can't talk, it's kind of inevitable that we can't make our innermost feelings known easily, if at all. That might be the sad reality, but I don't think it calls for all-out despair. Why? Because we "nonverbals" have a friend who lives inside us. Inhabiting my mind is a person who is Me and yet isn't Me. I talk to my other me as if he were an old friend, both when I'm happy and when I'm sad. This is why it's especially important never to hate ourselves. Once you start hating yourself, this old companion draws away. It's not easy to maintain your self-esteem if you're constantly feeling removed from your ideal self.

So. Please go ahead and tell us nonverbals "I like you" or "I love you" whenever the fancy takes you. When someone tells you that, it becomes a whole lot easier to like yourself.

## "IT CAN'T BE HELPED"

To be able to say about the past,
"It can't be helped," takes a certain
maturity of mind. At long last

I've arrived at the point where
I, too, can think: "You know?
That simply can't be helped."

For many, "It can't be helped"
might seem like a surrender.
For me, it signifies hope.

Back when I couldn't think this way,
I would obsess instead and
meltdowns would take over.

My "It can't be helped" speaks
of a future; a future that says,
"You know? Things are okay —

as they are."

## 45

# ANGER

Some people with autism go into a meltdown at the very sight of someone else getting a major scolding. Because of this, neurotypical people arrive at the conclusion that we hate the sight of anyone else getting into trouble and being shouted at. My take on this, however, is that the real reason the person with autism is shaken up so badly is because they are experiencing the scene as one where *they* are getting blamed for their own flaws and defects. I don't mean that he or she is suffering a flashback or that there is any confusion over who is in trouble. Nor do I think that any meltdown is rooted in an inability to help their friend in trouble, or arising from empathy. My theory is that witnessing the anger is a trigger for a panic attack, which then snowballs into a full meltdown as the neuro-atypical onlooker gets trapped in a spiral of self-loathing for having had a panic attack in the first place. Nobody's accusing them of anything at all, but they nonetheless experience blame and suffer the full stress. As for the reason why the person being told off *is* being told off? I suspect it rarely enters the equation.

# 46

## LAUGHING

Even when somebody is laughing their head off in front of me, I find it very hard to laugh along with them. It's not that I fail to find what they're laughing at funny: it's that I literally can't do it, because the moment I see someone start laughing, I forget to join in—I become entranced by the sight of the other person's laughing face. Then, when I'm *not* looking at the laughing person, I become ensnared by the *sound* of them laughing. In this way it slips my mind that I ever wanted to laugh. Not being able to laugh while everyone else is falling about the place is isolating enough, but what makes me feel even lonelier is that my inability to laugh along with others leads people to assume that I don't share their feelings or humor.

There are other times when I find the difference between an angry person's face and their normal face utterly hilarious. I might even want to see the furious expression again so badly that I burst out laughing—despite the anger this generates. Over-the-top scoldings definitely backfire in my case.

It can be tricky, I guess, to make people with autism like mine understand why they are being told off, especially when we're very young. The scene in which we did something wrong simply doesn't mesh with the scene in which we're being reprimanded. No doubt it varies from person to person, but I suggest that if a neuro-atypical child has done something wrong, the best course of action is just to point the misdemeanor out. Coolly and calmly.

## 47

# THORNS IN THE HEART

When I was a small boy, I used to think I could catch up with everyone else simply by refusing to quit. But as I grew up, I came to understand that, because of my autism, there are some things that other people do which I will never master, no matter how hard I try. The memory of how this realization wounded my spirit remains in my heart like a thorn that cannot be extracted. I assumed this wound would be with me forever because damage done in the past cannot be remedied.

By tackling challenges one by one, however, I've grown to be able to do a number of things that I couldn't do when I was young, and nowadays I'm a lot sunnier. When I was younger only *I* knew how miserable I was and I'd curl up under my stone. People would try to comfort me, telling me, "Hey, it's not such a big deal"—but for me, it really *was* a big deal. These days, however, I can look back at those scenes and agree: no, it wasn't the end of the world. My wrongheadedness caused me to misinterpret what the people watching over me were saying.

It turns out that wounds in the memory *can* be remedied, after all. How great it felt to draw that thorn out of my heart.

# GRACE

I often cause trouble for other people. This sometimes makes me miserable. But however inconsolable I get, I usually find that by the following day the wound has pretty much healed over. It's thanks to this that I can carry on and function as normal. Whatever it was that happened, my family just acts as if nothing out of the ordinary had occurred. My family's attitude means that the only thing I need to be concerned about is myself and my attitude. Since I've reached adulthood, I've come to appreciate how lucky I am to live in an environment such as the one my family gives me. While we can often overcome our own hardships, doing something about the troubles of other people is a much taller order. But when I hear the laughter of my family I feel this bubble-like, evanescent sensation—it's like when I'm entranced by a really great picture book I love, set in a distant land, beyond borders. Joyful memories warm my heart even now, like the lullabies heard long ago. They might be buried deep inside me but they're there and they're priceless and life without them would be impossible.

# "THE ONLY FLOWER
# IN THE WORLD"

When the song "The Only Flower in the World" by the J-Pop band SMAP was a monster hit, the message I got from the lyrics was that everyone wants to bloom in their own unique way. Speaking for myself, however, I don't want to be a one-of-a-kind "Only Flower in the World"; I'd prefer to be the kind of flower you can find all over the world, in any old place. The title of the song drips with such melancholy! However beautiful it was, however much adoration it received, wouldn't "the only flower in the world" be unendurably lonely? Maybe the beauty of a flower exists only when there's an observer there to admire it, but to my way of thinking it's actually the commonest wildflowers, weeds like dandelions which you can find the world over and which nobody really gives a second glance to, that are the happiest. Perhaps the dandelions can only dream, *Someday, I'll catch someone's eye and they'll turn around and notice me, and then I'll know for sure that the most beautiful flower is me.* But I wonder whether it's actually the dreaming of this dream—rather than it ever coming true—that is where the real happiness lies.

## MY DREAM ME

A long time ago I used to dream that I was a neurotypical child. In these dreams I was forever laughing, chatting away and swapping jokes with my friends and family. My Dream Me forgot all about My Real Me here in the waking world. Then I would wake up and return to myself, but I'd be clueless about where I was or what on earth I was doing in this place. When I finally realized I'd been dreaming, I'd well up and tears would spill down my face.

Dreams can be cruel. Things unthinkable in reality can easily come to pass. Are there not moments when your eyes are open but you wonder if you're waking or dreaming? To me, it's as if I'm standing at the fork in a road of a double life, seized by inertia. But no matter how beautiful the dream is, I sooner or later get drawn back to reality. I rub my eyes and get up from my futon. Strangely, perhaps, even though I envy My Dream Me, these days it's a bit of a relief to get back to who I really am. I now know that My Dream Me is also a Fake Me, I guess. I might have longed once to become that neurotypical version of myself, but really it was only in the way a child would want to be the hero in a film. Dreams might let us see things afresh, but they are illusions. This world is my world. There is no other.

# GRATITUDE

The point
of gratitude

lies in first
feeling gratitude

that one owes
gratitude.

PART 6

# HANDLE
# WITH CARE

# 51

# HITTING MY HEAD AND BITING MY CLOTHES

When I fight the demands of my fixations, and when my urge to do what my fixation dictates and my determination to ignore it smash into each other, I can erupt into anger. When I erupt into anger, I start hitting my head. I want to take control of the situation, but my brain won't let me. Neurotypical people never experience this, I guess. My rage is directed at my brain, so without thinking anything through, I set about punching my own head. Once I've mastered a fixation, I'm able to set its demands aside, ignore what my brain is saying and act according to my own wishes and feelings. If people try to tell me off while I'm hitting myself, or to forcibly stop me doing it, or yell, "What are you *doing*?" at me, I become utterly dejected. The more frantic and desperate I become, the more I punch myself: by now, it's no longer about punishing my brain, it's about punishing myself for having lost the plot so woefully. If, however, people don't flip out at the sight of me and understand that I'm not fully in control at such times, their forbearance gives me the headspace to think that one way or another I have to stop myself. So the next time you see someone like me in mid-meltdown, I'd ask you to conduct yourself with this knowledge.

There are other times when I succumb to bitter emotions or when things overwhelm me, when quick as a flash I sink my teeth into the sleeve of whatever I'm wearing; and as I bite I emit these feral noises that have no meaning like "Wooooooh" or a high-pitched "E-heeeeee." They calm me down. Often, when I'm pent up or wound up, I simply can't defuse the situation and I get more and more agitated until I'm like a perilously overinflated balloon and even the tiniest thing will make me explode. By biting my sleeve with all the strength I can muster, it's like the air is slowly let out of the balloon and gradually I return to my usual calm self. Biting my own clothes really isn't cool, I know, but as things currently stand this is what I need to do to stay on top of my challenging behavior. My goal for the future is to control my meltdowns without resort to this somewhat drastic tactic.

52

## HELP

Some people have rather fixed ideas about how those of us with autism ought to be supported. If they were all as correct in their views as they believe, however, autism wouldn't still be causing all the challenges and difficulties it does. You meet people who tell us, "Nope, you're doing it all wrong"; and, "Every single person who attends *this* institute makes amazing progress"—but if the latter was really true, word would spread like wildfire and everyone everywhere with autism would have adopted the miracle method ages ago. Any given therapy method might well work to some degree for some people with autism, but no approach will work across the board for every person with the condition. By the same token, I don't claim for a second that everything I've written in my books applies to each and every neuro-atypical person.

When "help for special needs" is considered, everyday assistance or ideal environments are often raised. These matter, for sure, but in my opinion the vital aim is to nurture motivation. Not stamina for its own sake, nor patience for its own sake, nor programs offering instant results, but hope for the future, positivity about learning and practical skills. What matters to people with disabilities is how they can lead rewarding lives twenty or thirty years from now. Who knows? Trying new approaches might reveal new and better paths. I would like for the chance to acquire new experiences to be thought of not as a favor but as a right.

Special needs teachers and helpers who can evaluate the effects of the help they offer are truly awesome. In contrast, those who think of themselves as infallible never stop to consider that they themselves could be connected with a child's unwelcome behavior. Please reflect, often, upon what's going on. We are people, like you, and our moods swing along with circumstances, like yours. You'll see how and why if you stop and think. Help isn't just a matter of getting us through our daily routines without a meltdown. Help varies from person to person. The help we really need might not be the help that others are bent on giving us. Events do not follow a script. This is being human.

# 53

## REPRIMANDS

When I've fallen into a bad mental place and I'm furious at myself for having fallen there, here's how I'd like you to handle me. If I'm all agitated and grouchy, please let me work through it. If I'm kind of at war with myself over control of my emotions, nothing you say is going to get through to me. Please be calm and even-tempered when I'm mid-meltdown, and don't try to talk me out of it. Reprimanding me while I'm struggling to master emotions carries this real risk: the words you use can all too easily get tangled up with my anger and complaints, which in turn can create a new verbal fixation. Your words will then stir me up even more, and I'll be reacting to and provoked by them in spite of my best efforts. If I'm only battling my emotions, then the more often I experience them, the sooner I'll be able to exercise control. But if a new fixation or verbal obsession gets added, I'll be compelled to follow its script every time; and I'll be angrier, for longer. Finally, once I've come back to myself again, please just treat me as you normally do. Reproaching or punishing someone with autism for having a meltdown makes us miserable. Rather than working out what to tell us at times like these, we'd prefer it if you just maintained the same calm attitude.

When boundaries of behavior are set, it's crucial to respect those boundaries, but it's doubly crucial that the boundaries are appropriate and realistic for the person and context in the first place. Unwarranted praise for sticking to rules doesn't make us—as adults—pleased. Similarly, being told, "Ah, sure, we'll make an exception to the rules just this once, just for you" is confusing, if not dismaying. From time to time situations will come up where, for whatever reason, stress levels mount and rules get bent and you might need to look the other way for strategic reasons.

When we've broken a rule, it's not because we believed ourselves to be an exception to it. Usually, we had no choice in the matter. On these occasions, please omit the telling-off and say to us instead, "Let's try and do a little better next time, shall we? And remember, I'm on your side." If possible, please keep your attitude and your demeanor the same as it always is. We already feel bad about having messed up, and guilty about the nuisance we've caused for our family and the people around us. Believe me.

# 54

## COMFORT ZONES

The times when a person with autism is conscious of his or her autism varies from person to person, I think. When I'm at home I often almost forget the fact of my autism, but to step outside our house is to encounter a host of situations in which the differences between myself and others soon become impossible to ignore. Some people might point to this as further proof of the world's harshness, but that's not actually how I see it. For me, it's a matter of pace. When I'm at home I can go about my daily routines at my own speed and *this* is why I'm able to forget about my autism. Perhaps doing things "at my own speed" could be construed as selfishness or dawdling or loafing about, but my interpretation, as applied to people with autism, relates to feeling comfortable and secure. Because I can seem ill-mannered or be noisy, people might not think I care one way or the other about matters of comfort, but in fact I'm hypersensitive to these things. Whenever I get trapped in a loop of asking the same pointless question over and over, or whenever I laugh out loud at darkly inappropriate moments, I get exasperated with myself and think I'm just incurably useless, and I sink right down.

I encroach upon other people's comfort zones yet I remain acutely sensitive about my own, maybe because I can do nothing to modify my circumstances. Even if I'm having a really bad time of it and someone urges me to go off somewhere to cool down on my own, doing so isn't at all straightforward. These "bad times" can blow up out of nowhere and any safe place or chill-out room offered to me appears to my eyes as infinitely distant, even if it's right there in front of me. I know I can visit safe rooms when I'm on a break or just when I feel like it, but if I was able to go there by myself midway through a meltdown, I'd also be able to indicate that I need help. Unfortunately I can do neither.

I hope that, one day, caregivers and professionals will be able to help people whose autism prevents them from showing they need help *before* it's too late. That would be something.

# 55

# THREE THOUGHTS
# ON SPECIAL NEEDS

When a person goes off the rails mentally they cease to be their usual selves, it seems; yet even the person concerned has an inkling something really isn't right. This self-awareness strikes me as odd. If they know they're behaving strangely, they ought to be able to fix it, you'd think; and yet they can't. They suffer for this, surely. I wonder if they per-ceive what people with full-on autism like mine also per-ceive: that while mind and body appear to be interconnected, they are actually not, not as we experience them. I don't believe that people with special needs have wholly unique existences. People sometimes say that there is a lot to learn from those of us with special needs, but I don't think the positives should be the sole focus. There are kindhearted people in the world, and not so kindhearted ones, irrespec-tive of whether special needs enter the equation. To bring about equality for the neuro-atypical minority, we first need to dispel the illusions about us. We aren't angels, nor are we devils; we are just ordinary people.

Some people with autism object strongly to the use of the word *gai*, meaning "harm," in *shō-gai*, the Japanese word for disability, where *shō* means "obstacle." I understand where they're coming from, but I think that trying to impose their views on everyone else, whether they disagree or are just indifferent, is going too far. Such an unquestioning belief in their own correctness risks doing more harm than good.

Bringing up a child who has special needs *really* isn't an easy matter, and when the parents of these children find themselves unable to love their kid, I can't think of them as bad parents; rather, I blame the situation and its hardships. I also think it's only natural for them to wonder how things would be if their children didn't have any disabilities. There are times when I, too, think this way, and I no longer feel guilty about doing so. It's only a flight of fancy. The neurotypical Me in these daydreams always seems to be smiling, but I have no way of knowing if that Me is any happier than the Me I am in reality. Nobody in this world is free from worry.

# 56

# "GROOVED-IN" FAILURE

There are some children with autism who just aren't great at putting their things back in the correct place. Maybe they don't understand why they're the only ones being told off, even though they're putting their items back in the same general area as the others—especially if it's after the event.

To tackle this, I'd suggest helping the child put their things back in the correct spot—as often as is needed and *prior* to the child making the mistake. For example, a moment before the putting away begins, confirm that he or she knows exactly which name, symbol, label or sticker designates the right location for the object. Here's why this matters so much: for children with autism, failure counts as a life experience, so repeated failure gets "grooved in." Neurotypical children learn from their mistakes and failures, but some children—us—can only learn by repeating an action correctly, over and over. Further explanations with extra details won't help, I'm afraid. There are many ways to get something wrong, but usually there's only one way to get it right, so to help the child to understand what that right way is, it's by far best to teach and to show *only* the correct way. Adults with a teaching role seek to enable us, so we can do the things we can't—yet being told off for failing at the same task every day is a deeply negative experience, and in front of our friends and classmates, it's even worse. Remember, our feelings are as readily bruised as yours.

Bearing the above in mind, when I've done something wrong, I *do* want to know about it. Otherwise, people won't recognize me as a valid person and, at best, they'll just feel pity for me. For sure, there'll be things I can't do even after you've shown me where I've gone wrong again and again— but that doesn't mean I won't be able to manage them someday. When you encounter a child who reacts resentfully to guidance, I'd guess they've been disciplined in the past in ways that taught them they were a waste of space, or plain bad. Even young children understand when they're being scolded for a genuine wrong, I think. Some of them will be feeling terrible because they know they're in the wrong but can't see a way to remedy it. I believe that all children wish to grow and embrace their futures. Please nurture this wish.

# 57

# "EVERYBODY'S DOING THEIR BEST!"

I must admit, a part of me shrivels up inside whenever I hear the stock phrase, "Everybody's doing their best!" Why? First off, "Everybody's doing their best" is rarely a statement of fact. Usually it's truer to say, "Everybody *looks like* they're doing their best." Looking like you're doing your best is all well and good, but let's not simply assume that it's the reality. Next, I have a problem with the idea that just because everyone else is doing their best, I have to do so as well— that strikes me as artificial. Of course, there's nothing wrong with doing something as best you can, and I'm not wallowing in self-pity, because often even my autistic best is beyond my capabilities on the day. The point is that to declare "Everybody's doing their best!" ends up forcing comparisons of "bests," which in turn feels unfair and pointless.

When someone tells me, "Keep up the good work," I'm duly grateful, and if they tell me, "Stick at it!" I know they're showing me that they're on my side. Having your strenuous efforts acknowledged can fortify you and spur you on. However, we are all only human, and there are going to be times when "doing our best" simply isn't an option. This needs to be allowed for, too. The degree of effort we put into a task should be determined by us.

Compassionate people understand that being told to "Do your best!" can feel like an extra burden, or come across as an exhortation to up one's game. "Do your best" isn't a harmful phrase in and of itself, but it's wise to remember that there are some words and phrases which some people, quite legitimately, are happiest not using or hearing.

# 58

# PLODDING ALONG,
# TORTOISE-LIKE

When I'm practicing something every day but I'm still getting nowhere, I feel like I'm plodding along, tortoise-like. *Absolutely anyone can do this, so why can't I?* My ongoing failure weighs heavily. It's taken for granted that in order to acquire the skills we don't have, we need to practice every day—this is why the people who work with us pay such close attention to the results of our practice. But for those of us actually doing the practicing, often the process doesn't feel like the natural, obvious way of doing things at all. We're always being told, "It's fine to progress toward your goals a tiny bit at a time"—but this is our therapists and helpers talking, not us. We, who are putting the practice in, want to master whatever we're doing as soon as possible. Having us take these incremental steps might feel right and look correct for the neurotypical people around us, but those of us who are being obliged to work at a snail's pace might be sighing inwardly at our slow progress toward new goals. Anyone—neurotypical or not—can tell whether they're getting better at something. Or not. Surely?

My point: please don't think that by *not* pushing someone toward a goal or by *not* stretching their abilities, you're automatically making it easier for them to arrive. Life isn't that great for turtles, and plodding along tortoise-like is no picnic either.

# CURIOSITY

Somewhere, sometime, someone
is expecting us; so we suspect.

Here we stand at the heart
of the world; so we like to think.

Self-regarding animals, we human
beings; and *curious*. I suspect

however weak we are, however
grueling our lives, this is why

we carry on.

# 59

# INGRAINED FIXATIONS

My fixations can hang around a long time before they disappear. However much effort I put into trying to free myself from these obsessive behaviors, they remain really stubborn. You—our minders, teachers, guardians—can act like nothing's wrong, or you can threaten to punish us if we don't stop or offer to reward us if we do, but the fact is that some fixations are nearly impossible to get around. Maybe some people with autism derive comfort from them, but my guess is that most of us want them to stop, and suffer because we can't make them go away. Speaking for myself, the only cure I know is for you to give us—and our fixations—time.

You can help by staying with us as we work through our fixations, by not reproaching us too much for exhibiting them and by maintaining an unswerving belief that one day we will be free of them. Because they don't last forever. Even the most ingrained fixation can just up and vanish, as if some demonic curse has lifted itself. I can't explain how or why they go when they go, but I know that once an obsessive fixation has departed, it leaves me in a state of perfect bliss.

Naturally, people in our lives point our obsessive behaviors out to us because they want us to stop doing them. But I would ask you not to reprimand us in ways that damage our dignity. Believe me: the biggest victim of a fixation is the person who suffers from it.

# 60

# THE GIFT OF CHOICE

It's vital, I believe, that those of us who live with autism are permitted to exercise choice independently. Even after I became able to choose items on my own, my mother would, without fail, check with me: "Look, there's this one, this one and this one—which would you like?" She would ask me to point to the one I wanted and confirm my choice yet again by having me spell it out on her palm or my alphabet grid. Mom's asking me to state my choice twice cost her extra effort, but for me it mattered very much. My outer expressions don't always correspond to my inner intentions, so it was really important to practice expressing my wishes correctly. In fact, it was thanks to these opportunities my mother gave me to choose between objects that I recently worked out why I sometimes select an option at odds with the one I really intended to choose: it can be because an aspect of the object seizes my attention, or a leading phrase in the question is swaying my choice, or I'm being influenced by a question-and-answer pattern that is "pre-fixed" in my head.

Whenever I have to select something, my mind kind of goes blank. When I'm instructed to "pick something," the urgency of having to do so throws me into a tailspin. If I'm told, "Come *on,* choose one of them!" then the only thing that matters is that I have to choose one, right now. I guess for neurotypical people there is pleasure to be found in making a choice, but this is not a luxury that I can enjoy. However, since I've learned to communicate my thoughts and wishes to some degree by writing on palms or via my grid, I am at least able to reset my decision if I make a wrong choice. I'm also better able to consider why I went for the option I didn't want, work out which one I should have chosen, and let people around me know which option is the right one for me, after all.

To those of you who live, work or deal with people who have nonverbal autism, I recommend switching the order of the items on offer and sidestepping the "triggers" of fixed responses. This will help you ascertain which option the person with autism *genuinely* wants. It's also crucial that people who work with us steer clear of bias and preconceived notions about our choices and don't fall into the trap of thinking, *this one here is the one he needs!* Remember that the very same person can vary his or her choice depending on how they feel that day, and that our preferences can change with the seasons, or as we just get older.

Finally, please be mindful that, with the best will in the world, while you are intending to give us a free choice, you might inadvertently be swaying us one way or the other.

# 61

# WHAT WOULD YOU LIKE TO BE?

When you were small, I'm sure you were often asked, "And what would you like to be when you grow up?" This question is rarely put to children with disabilities. Not, I think, because people don't expect the child to understand, but because they assume it to be the parent's or therapist's responsibility to map out the child's future, not the child's. To my mind, however, it's vital for any child to be able to dream about who and what they'd like to be and do in their future. The answer doesn't have to involve a profession—more than any answer, it's the act of imagining that really counts. Tomorrow might be indistinguishable from yesterday, but on the far side of tomorrow the whole of our future is waiting, and it's our present selves who dream that future into being. So please, next time, go ahead and ask children with special needs what they'd like to be in the future. By asking, you're enabling them to look forward to it with pleasure.

# AN ALPHABET INTERVIEW

IN *THE BIG ISSUE* BY ITS VENDORS AND STAFF
(APRIL 2015)

PART 2: N TO Z

**N:** If a replacement word for autism—*jiheisho*—were to be coined, what would you like it to be?

I can understand why some people would like *jiheisho*—"self-locked-up disease"—to be changed, but personally speaking, I can live with the word. Changing the name of a disability would take a vast amount of energy and I'd prefer it if these resources were applied to making our society a more autism-friendly place.

**O:** How would you define "being independent"?

The knowledge that I am a valid member of society, in a financial sense as well as a social one.

**P:** We're the same age, you and me. What do you think of our generation of young people?

A person isn't of more or less interest to me just because we're of the same generation. The same applies to a person's thoughts. All the way down human history it seems that older generations have grumbled about younger ones being impossible to understand. Young people, myself included, are products of the society we belong to. What I'm curious about is how other generations perceive ours.

Q: What we think, what we like and what we believe varies widely from person to person. How do you suggest people with so many diverse ideas can live harmoniously?

People shouldn't think they *have* to be friends with others, but if they can acknowledge each other's cultures, and respect each other as valid human beings, this is enough, I think. Because we try to build friendly relations with others, we expect them to understand us. Our interest can end up with us trying to know more about them than is required or tactful. Religions and ways of life are ingrained into us from the beginning. In the end, we might try to force ideas onto each other. Coexisting as we do matters most.

R: More's the pity, there are calculating, hurtful people in the world, but I like to believe they were born kind and good. How do you think their original gentler selves can be restored?

I don't think that anyone's born kind or good. What we become is learned and formed later, and only if a person wishes to be compassionate can he or she become compassionate. Perhaps those same calculating, hurtful people might show kindness toward those who are precious to them. All we can do is to offer help to any tricked or damaged victims.

**S:** You wrote some poems about war. What kind of society would you like to see in the future?

I'm sure everyone would like to see an end to war. Fighting solves nothing: all we end up with are winners and losers. Despite the truth of this, why people never stop waging wars is something I'll always wonder about.

**T:** Do you still feel an affinity with the wind, "dissolve" into sunlight or listen to flowers or trees? Can I do it too?

Unfortunately, I'm less connected to nature than I used to be. If asked whether I miss that affinity, I'd say yes, I do. However, I've grown fonder of myself as a human being, so maybe it's for the best. After all, a person can't really live as the wind—but at least we can listen to its voice.

**U:** You've said, "To me, human beings aren't attractive." If you could be reincarnated as something else, what would it be?

There are so many things I'd like to be, it's difficult to choose one! But for now, I'll say a cat. There's no obvious reason why, but I suspect that I'd have a lot more freedom as a cat.

**V:** What does "God" mean to you?

I don't believe in one specific religion but I acknowledge the existence of God as a superlative entity beyond words.

**W:** What kind of books do you read?

The books I usually read are the picture books I've been reading since I was a boy, though the writer who has influenced me most is Kenji Miyazawa. Of the stories my mother read me back then, his *Night on the Galactic Railroad* moved me the most.

**X**: What are words for you? Do you have a favorite?

For me, words are bridges that connect me with others. It's impossible for me to make myself understood facially or visually. The letter that is special to me is の [pronounced "no" as in "not"] because of its beautiful curve. My favorite word is 希望 [*kibou*; pronounced "key-bor"]—hope.

**Y**: Last year you were invited to the U.S. to give a presentation. What made the biggest impression on you? Would you like to visit any other countries?

What impressed me most in the U.S. was their understanding about autism. It's much more advanced there. Even at a museum, a guard allowed me to follow a fixation without forcing me to obey the rules that other visitors had to. Thanks to the goodwill of Americans I met, I could travel without suffering any major panic attacks. If the chance comes along, I'd love to visit Europe one day.

**Z**: You've written poems, essays, children's books, fables and picture books. Do your thoughts and feelings change depending on what you're writing? How did you learn to write such elegant, precise and flowing sentences that touch your readers so gently? What kind of techniques and practices do you employ?

Whatever form I write in, my thoughts and feelings are the same. I just hope that my writing finds a readership. If I can make any kind of impression upon my readers, then as a writer I'll feel honored. What I pay attention to while I'm writing is not to overexplain things; and to write those things that I, and only I, can write. These two objectives may look easy, but in fact they are both highly demanding tasks. My ideal is that a single sentence I write can evoke many and varied images in the mind of the reader.

PART 7

**AWAY**

# 62

# THE GATE

When I was a small boy, I used to stop at a certain gate whenever we passed by it. This gate had an ornamental latch with a lion's face on it, which I enjoyed looking at. At first—so she tells me—Mom had no idea why I used to suspend our walk in front of a total stranger's house. But one day, when the lion latch had swiveled upside down, I tried to put it back the right way up, and then Mom figured out what was going on. She told me that you can't just go touching other people's gates without permission, so I did my best to twist my head around so the lion would at least appear to be the right way up.

Looking back, I really can't say why the lion on the gate fascinated me as much as it did. Perhaps I just thought, *Wow, a lion on a gate—how cool is that?* When neurotypical kids are interested in something, they can satisfy their curiosity simply by putting their question to the nearest adult before moving on to the next thing, and the next, and the next. Back then, however, I couldn't ask anyone anything. My fascinations remained locked up in my head. Like time was standing still.

# 63

## ENTRY PROHIBITED

There are times when I stand in front of doors or places you can't enter and say in a loud voice, "Entry prohibited!" Or when I see a flowerbed, I can't help but call out, "Don't walk in there!" or "You'll trample on the flowers!" while lifting one foot. None of this is about verifying whether or not these actions are allowed; rather, it's to remind myself that I mustn't do these things. I understand well enough what I can or can't do, but when something captivates me, or when I get excited, it can get a little challenging to steer my actions. Because of this, I speak directly to my brain. I access the words or scenes that made an impression on me and vow to myself not to do anything that might be considered out of place. This might look ridiculous to other people, but it's how I stay in control of things best.

Because I have difficulty managing my speech and behavior, I live with a sense of resignation about things I've done in the past. It's hard for me to explain my actions or to start things over from the beginning. Thanks to this, I've had my fair share of sad experiences. However, I've learned that neurotypical people are also tormented by past events. Human words and actions, I've come to understand, often go hand in hand with emotional pain.

Even when you've made a blunder, I don't want you to beat yourself up about it. I think if we can acknowledge all the variations of who we are, we can also be at peace with who we were in the past. Perhaps, by at least *trying* to stay on the right path, we humans won't go too far wrong.

64

## PAYING

When I pay for things in shops, I can't always just hand over the money—sometimes it can take me forever. I'm a bit on the clumsy side anyway, but the main reason here is that I try to pay the exact amount. I know that it's perfectly okay to hand over more than the total price and to get some change back—it doesn't have to be the exact amount—but as soon as I see the price flash up on the cash register, my mind fixates upon handing over that precise amount of money. There are people who might advise me to pay with a thousand-yen note every time I buy something, but then *that* could become a new fixed pattern of behavior and the whole idea of receiving change could start to throw me. For example, I might ask for change when buying items that come to a thousand yen exactly, or that cost more than a thousand yen—and then get angry if I don't receive it. This is why I practice paying the exact amount—or maybe a little bit more, to be on the safe side.

# EATING OUT

One time I went out with my dad to an Indian restaurant. The naan bread was amazing. Dad asked me, "So how's the naan?" and "Is the curry too hot, or is it just right?" It was nice that he was thinking about my enjoyment of the meal, but if I'm honest, I wasn't much thinking about the menu or how our dishes tasted. To me, the most pressing matters were the fact that we had come out to a restaurant I hadn't been to before and my anxiety over how I could finish the meal without bothering the other diners. The food was a secondary issue.

Most people go to a restaurant to be served and to eat, but my main concern is whether they'll let me in or not. Because family dinner outlets and fast-food joints are identical wherever you go, I'm familiar with the atmosphere and decor before I even enter—this is very calming. Eating out at new restaurants is much more of a challenge, but I want to broaden my experience. I'll keep trying.

# WANTING TO VANISH

Some people who have autism don't like being seen, so they hide their faces behind clothing or blankets. My case was a little different: my motive for running off when I was younger was that I hated myself so much that I didn't want anyone else even to see me. I'm guessing this isn't easy for you to understand, but I yearned to vanish from the world. This wasn't quite the same thing as wanting to be dead. It wasn't that I hated the world, or life; it was a severe inability to accept myself for who and what I was.

Yet at the same time, I was also convinced that one day someone would come along and rescue me from everything. All I wanted was to hide myself away until that day arrived. My reasoning was that if I couldn't see anybody, nobody could see me. In fact I only reached a place where I'm okay with being seen when I was able, finally, to accept my disability.

When I'm in shops or traveling I am often surrounded by strangers. I'm not good at handling these situations and they make me uneasy—not because of any strong urge to go home or because I don't know what to do, but because of a fear that my unease could get badly out of hand and turn into a major inconvenience for other people. Maybe there's not a lot I can do about this, but if I spend my life avoiding crowds because of a fear of what *might* happen, I'll never be able to go anywhere. I need a whole array of tactics, I feel, but what I can do is practice. People with special needs shouldn't give up. We should make sure we get out of the house. I'll do my best, too.

# 67

# CHAOS IN THE BRAIN

On a day of heavy snow my mother and I had planned to go to Tokyo. Midway, however, the train we were on was declared out of service. My mother figured we weren't going to be able to reach our destination and decided to turn back. I'd never been in that situation before, and it became a very challenging situation. I *knew* the best course of action was to head for home, but I just couldn't take this idea on board. What was going on?

When it comes to sudden changes of plan, I need to obtain my brain's consent. It takes work to accommodate my feelings to the change. I can't simply tell myself, *If we don't turn back we'll end up getting stuck in the snow; and anyway, we can always go another time.* In a case like the one above, the trick was mentally to edit our destination. The action of boarding the train and what I'd do at our destination were unrelated. Of course it was a shame that we couldn't arrive there as planned, but what my brain really got hung up on was not how I felt about the change, but the fact that I wouldn't be able to confirm—with my own eyes—our arrival at the planned destination on the station signboard. So in order to avert a meltdown, I needed to alter the original station name in Tokyo that my brain had already memorized to the name of the halfway station where my mother and I got off the train instead.

I managed to vocalize the change by naming the station and adding, "Left the train." And my mother replied, "Yes, that's right—we got off the train at such-and-such a station, didn't we?" It was a bit like updating a computer file. By reciting this exchange many times, I was able to calm myself down. This is what helps me when I'm subject to confusion of this sort—being told off or ignored really doesn't help at all. In the end, it dawned on me: in these situations, the source of all my difficulties is chaos in the brain.

# 68

## MISUNDERSTANDINGS

One of the hardest things for anyone is probably being unable to straighten out misunderstandings. In general, people are aware of how tricky it is for those of us with autism to express ourselves, but how about our inability to offer explanations or excuses? Our autistic traits tend to multiply misunderstandings by making us do things we didn't really intend or blurt out sounds and words we didn't really want to, or by preventing us from apologizing when we'd really like to. Nothing is harder than finding yourself steered into a situation you can't properly explain your way out of . . .

I give presentations all over Japan, but whenever I find myself at a new train station I always feel distinctly uneasy. It's like the way I could never stay still the day before a school excursion and would keep pacing around, on edge. The more I think *I have to stay on top of this,* the more fiercely my obsessions or fixations are ignited. Anyway, my station obsession compels me to go looking through the station's souvenir shops for confectionery or merchandise or anything emblazoned with a famous cute kitten character decked out in local clothes and objects. Once I've found it, I don't buy it—all I have to do is point a finger at it and declare, "There it is!" and I'm satisfied. Perhaps this is close to what other people feel when they grip a good-luck charm from a shrine before an important exam.

One time, after I'd already gone through the ticket barrier, I badly needed to retrace my steps to the souvenir shop I'd just left. Of course, I know you're not allowed just to breeze back through a ticket barrier at a train station, but on that occasion I *really* had to go and see those items one more time—I had no say in this whatsoever—so I went back out of the gate I'd just gone through. The onlookers were pretty shocked: I'd barged out the wrong way without asking permission from the station staff. Very soon, a station officer caught up with me to demand an explanation, but all I could do was shriek the name of the kitten character over and over. To make matters worse, by now the officer was telling me, "Stay where you are—don't move, please!" while I was trying to dash off to the souvenir shop. Just when I'd thrown that area of the station into complete chaos, my mother emerged from the stall where she'd been buying our lunch, noticed the commotion and came running. She explained to the station officer about my disability and the matter was soon settled. After that, we returned to the shop, I confirmed the kitten character was still where she belonged, we went back through the ticket barrier and got onto our bullet train without further ado.

So: people with autism might talk and behave in peculiar-seeming ways, but this shouldn't relegate us to a lesser branch of humanity. Please give us the benefit of the doubt and act on the assumption that we're good people. If you suspect we're a lost cause, we pick up on that. The value of a person shouldn't be decided by the judgments of other people. Kindness brings out the best in us all.

## SAY "CHEESE!"

I'm not good at having my photograph taken. Staring at the camera is difficult for me, even when my eyes are being directed by someone pointing and telling me, "Look at the camera! Right there!" I wonder if you can guess why? It's because whenever I hear the word "camera" I run through my mental store of ideas about cameras in an attempt to match them with one I can see in front of me. It's not quite that a concrete image of a camera floats into my mind; rather, that I try to find common matching aspects between my *notions* of cameras and the one in my visual field. What I get back is, *No, that's not right* and *No, this isn't right, either.*

I know very well what a camera is, but when one is put in front of me it sort of stops being a camera and is transformed into some tool-like object. What's more, if I'm also instructed to "smile!" or "lower your chin a little" or "rest your hands on your knees" I get totally thrown.

No, I'm *really* not good at having my photograph taken.

# TRAVELING

I love going away to different places, but often I'm unable to let the people around me know this. I might be happy inside, but because I can't visualize how I'll handle being in the new place, I end up having a meltdown or crying and getting overly emotional about even quite trivial things. Neurotypical people don't suffer from misunderstandings about whether they are happy or not, I think, because they can explain their emotions using words. At times like this I get really sad. When I create trouble for the people I'm with, I become afraid that they'll start to regret bringing me to the place and that I won't be allowed out again. It drives me to despair!

My mom, however, knows what I'm feeling and keeps smiling even as she apologizes for me to the people around us. "That was amazing, wasn't it?" she says to me. Even if I messed everything up and things totally went to pieces, it'll be, "Let's go back again, shall we?" In the past, I never handled hotels and new places very well, but these days I'm slowly getting used to it. In fact, going on vacation is one of my biggest pleasures. I encounter landscapes that I don't normally see and just by having a change of scene I sometimes feel that I've become a brand new me.

Traveling with people who have special needs might present difficulties, but please, let it happen. We all need a break and a change of scene sometimes. This is as true for us as it is for you. Being in a new environment can be confusing, but one by one the challenges can be addressed and new things can be experienced. It's thanks to travel, to encountering new people and being helped by their kindness, that I've been made aware of how fantastic life can be. There is a fixed idea that one's surroundings are everything there is: I've come to learn that this fixed idea narrows and limits the way we see things. The vastness of the world is a source of inspiration. Don't you think?

## FLYING

*Wouldn't it be great to fly?*
Everyone dreams this once
at least. But I wonder if it's not
flying over endless skies
we want but rather to be free
of all the stuff down here, below.

Yet
what if

freedom is not a matter of
leaving things behind, but of
bringing inside what is out. By
opening up the door of the heart,
we take a step toward the world.
Step by step by step by step we might,
one day, hold freedom in our hands.

# NEW YORK

I was aware of Japan and New York's thirteen-hour time difference, but because I have a real fixation about time, my mom was anxious about how I'd cope. In the event, I didn't get as confused as we'd expected. On the in-flight entertainment screen there were two clocks, one for Japan time and one showing the time in New York. It's strange to think of two times existing simultaneously, but as long as my schedule and actions have one time reference, that's enough and I'm okay; deciding which clock to synch up with didn't faze my brain at all. Until I fell asleep on the airplane, I was on Japan time. After I woke up, I switched to New York time. This wasn't a tip we'd followed or a plan we'd made—it just made sense when I saw the two clocks. Actually, the toughest part was the jet lag. I was sleepy during our entire stay in New York. At our hotel I slept way more than I usually do, and my head was in a groggy round-the-clock haze—which might explain my heightened sense of New York being a dream. Not yawning in front of people is a challenge at the best of times, so I'm afraid that I might have seemed ruder than usual to Americans when I was over there . . .

Even in New York, thanks to my severe autism, I was the source of stress and inconvenience for many people—as usual. Naturally this wasn't fun for me either, but on a couple of occasions, despite being in a new city, things went better and more smoothly than they might have done in Japan. On our visit to the Metropolitan Museum of Art, I wandered off the main route through an exhibition and tried to enter a room I wasn't supposed to go into at that point. A staff member stopped me, but as soon as my mom and our translator explained about my autism, the museum employee said, "Oh, in that case, go ahead, no problem"—just as if he was a special needs assistant with a good understanding of autism—and waved us through with a friendly smile. If this had happened in a museum in Japan, it's much likelier that the staff member would have told me, "Wait here, please," and gone off to consult with a supervisor, leaving me in limbo for the duration. My agitation levels would have risen until I was making high-pitched noises like a kettle on a stove, before I boiled over into a meltdown. At times like these, all I want is to see, close up, the artifact that caught my eye—I'm not going to touch it or hassle anyone. I know museums have viewing routes, I know museum staff are right to ask visitors to follow them and I know that I should, too; but sometimes this is simply not an option available to me and I need a little flexibility to break the impasse my autism puts me in. Back at the Metropolitan Museum I looked at the artwork I needed to see, and then rejoined the regular route. Truly, I don't want VIP treatment. I just want the chance to enjoy extraordinary art and artifacts and have my mind enriched by them. Like anybody else.

English feels like an old friend to me. I've always been fascinated by its directness and its rhythmic beauty, so being surrounded by English in New York didn't feel all that alienating. Despite my liking for the language and having a reasonable vocabulary, I can't use my alphabet grid to communicate in it, perhaps because I lack exposure to English in my daily life. If I listened to everyday English more in Japan, maybe I could remedy this. Just memorizing set phrases, as we all know, isn't that much practical use when you want to speak with someone.

I was taken aback by the vastness of New York. The city gave me the impression of an entire country made up of many peoples and cultures. People there believe everyone has the chance to succeed. Maybe this stems from a deep-seated desire to understand others rather than to exclude them. I saw the Statue of Liberty from the water. As I watched her, standing upright and reaching into the sky, I was very moved and thought how I would like to live my life the same way. New York intensified my desire to see the wider world and showed me how narrow was the world I'd known before I went. What I took in with my eyes in New York, what I heard with my ears and felt with my skin, I wish to swap for words. Words I wish to write down. Words I wish to send on their way.

PART 8 | **HOME**

# 72

# HOME

When my family is relaxed and enjoying downtime together at home, I'm at my happiest. I might not be able to join in with their conversation, and from my face and reactions you wouldn't know that I'm enjoying myself, but just watching my family being a family brings me great pleasure. The times I feel I *most* belong with them are when they've noticed some slight change in me. I also love it when I laugh at something on cue and they say, "Hey, Naoki found that funny!" I'm elated when this happens: it's normally so hard for me to show what I'm feeling in a normal, natural way. Or when we're dividing up some snacks and they say, "Which one takes your fancy, Naoki?" At times like these I feel a palpable sense of being a part of my family. It's just great.

I yearn to pass as an ordinary person you'd not give a second glance to. I doubt most people can imagine what it's like to be noticed and watched the whole time, but when I'm with my family at home, they don't pay overly close attention to me. My mom and my sister chat away, everyone does their own thing, or house-type jobs, or watches TV . . . and I get to be an ordinary person. Being at home helps me keep a grip on things and brings me peace of mind. My self-esteem benefits, too, from the fact that I'm never given special treatment in our house. I have no memory of ever being singled out at home, or being guilt-tripped.

I've been brought up in my family with full membership and I think that because of this I aspire to live in society without being treated as a special case all the time. My family gives me a place to belong, with attendant roles and responsibilities. I'm neither a princeling nor a spare part, and if we people with special needs belong in our families as a matter of course, is there not hope that one day we'll create a place in the wider world where we belong, too?

# 73

# PICTURE BOOKS

Sometimes my helper and I go to the local library, where I sit myself down in the children's section and go through picture books. The ones I read are pretty much always the same; in fact, since childhood, the repertoire has hardly altered. I prefer to think this is not owing to limited intelligence; rather, it's because when I read them, my mind goes wandering off inside the world of the picture book and I can freely, safely, unwind. Here in the real world, there aren't many places where I and my autism can lower our guard. Like flowing water or the texture of sand or the beauty of light, my favorite picture books afford me a therapeutic comfort.

When I was really little, oddly enough, picture books left me cold. Mom would try to read them to me but I'd just run off—it really did her head in! My knowledge of words was so scant that my mother reading a picture book to me was just another noise—like the sound of lots of people talking all at once. Picture books might look very simple but they require imagination to work; and since I showed zero response to any picture book of any kind, I caused my mother a great deal of worry—so I'm now told. One day, however, she noticed how often I was looking through old photographs. So Mom put together a photo book using our family pictures, and wrote short sentences alongside the images. It was thanks to this that the whole point of picture books "clicked" for me, and from then on the number that I enjoyed steadily grew. Also, I could begin to relate my everyday self to the characters in the books.

Conventional wisdom has it that people with autism have little interest in other people and little understanding of other people's emotions. I'm no longer so sure about this. One day, I suddenly became aware that Mom wasn't around and—jolted—I set off in search of her. She was only upstairs, but she was surprised that I'd come looking for her. Previous to this, it had always been my mother who was wondering where *I* had wandered off to. I'd never searched for anyone else out of anxiety for them as opposed to wanting something from them. I had always existed in a world with just one principal character, much like the world of a picture book. Life for people with autism can be like this, and if only a day could pass as effortlessly as the turning of a page, we would be content. However, this isn't the same as being incapable of compassion or sympathy. The Naoki who was worrying about where Mom had gone was a Naoki who had jumped out of that picture-book existence. I know I'll never be like anyone else straightaway—if ever—but little by little, I intend to write my own story.

# RESPECT

My family earns my respect. Not because they're enlightened beings, but because, very simply, they're there for me, they wish me the best, and they accept me for who I am. That might sound run-of-the-mill but I know well how taxing it is to share a life with me and this disability known as autism. My family gets stony glares from strangers and they're messed around by my fixations, panic attacks and meltdowns, but they never turn their backs on me. They're used to these things; end of story. Thanks to this "water off a duck's back" attitude, they show me hope for the future, lift me out of passive resignation and help me understand that my lot in life isn't so freakishly out of the ordinary after all.

Everyone ought to be worthy of respect. The word evokes reverence—an image of admiring a person, or of striving to emulate them. In my case, however, the people I respect outside my family are those who have taught me various things as I've moved through life. Schoolmaster-type instruction leaves me a little cold: what impresses me more is how a person lives his or her life.

## MOM

My mother is unshakable. She looks like any other mom, but nothing can faze her. Even when things go horribly pear-shaped, she never kicks up a fuss or loses her head. She just accepts and embraces my feelings and responses. I think this is why I can speak with her about anything, anything at all. Mom's number one goal in life seems to be to make my family laugh. She praises me and my sister to the skies when we've done or said something funny; if we've done housework or if we've been studying, all we'll get is a "Thanks!" or a "Well done"—though this, too, she says from the heart, so I'm still warmed by her words.

I hear it said sometimes that for very young children with autism, even the notion of having parents might not register. In my case, too, I only became aware that my parents *were* my parents at a later stage than my neurotypical peers. I guess you might think this makes it harder for a parent-child bond to form, but I disagree. A child might not know what a "parent" is exactly, but we are filled and ingrained, I believe, with the love our parents have poured into us. My mother might once have been just a "useful person" but I grew to appreciate how devoted she is. Sentiments such as *I'll love my child when his mind is maturer* or *She doesn't understand anything so she can't feel love* are way off the mark. Way off the mark.

# 76

## MY SISTER AND I

I like hanging out in my sister's room. She never shoos me away. We don't necessarily interact—I just enjoy her company. Often she's studying or reading magazines at her desk, while I sit on the floor leafing through picture books or doing number games. Being with her like this is more fun than being on my own and I'm really thankful for this place, right here in my big sister's room, where I'm never rejected or get special treatment.

I've heard people say that it's difficult to raise siblings without betraying any favoritism at all, but I'm not so sure that siblings really want identical treatment. What they want to feel is an equality of love. If I didn't feel this in our house, then regardless of whether I was being treated better than my sister or more shoddily, I'd still feel a sense of grievance toward our parents. But I feel my sister and I are loved equally, especially when I see her getting on well with Mom and Dad, and looking happy to be here. My sister is my mirror, in one sense. If she wasn't comfortable at home, I couldn't be. Happiness that comes at someone else's expense isn't happiness—especially if that someone else is precious to you. Even when I have to monopolize our mom's time, my sister doesn't get jealous—she knows that we're concentrating and working, and not just idling the day away.

Every single one of us has roles to fulfill and challenges to face, and none of us is a hero, not on close examination. My family has its share of difficulties, just like any other. But it's this equality of love that my sister and I both feel from our parents which lets us feel at home, at home.

# 77

## DAD

Fathers—if present—play a key role in family life, and ir-respective of whether he's a loving and active dad, a worka-holic, not much interested in raising the kids or living with a long-term illness, for better or for worse, your father's your father and you only have the one. I rarely talk about my fa-ther in a public forum like this. He's a company employee, so I don't want to create any awkwardness or embarrass-ment for him. Lots of people I've met are curious about how my father interacts with me, but I wouldn't say he's done anything all that out of the ordinary. While my mother and my sister keep an eye on me around the clock, my dad doesn't have that much to say about what I might or might not be up to. When he's home he likes to read the paper or watch the news on TV. If there's a report that captures his attention, he'll discuss it with us at some length. What really piques his interest is whether statistics are being used misleadingly, or where an argument is contradicting itself. He's very good at pointing these instances out. Dad had a technical education and he finds it unforgivable when data is oh-so-conveniently misinterpreted and dodgy "findings" are proclaimed as self-evident truths. My father's opinions keep me on my toes. He talks about what happens behind the scenes in society and about half-hidden episodes in history, and he airs points of view that can differ markedly from my mother's and sister's. While my dad's talking you might not guess from my general demeanor that I'm listening attentively—but I am.

What I've learned from my father is that society is composed of diverse types of people who hold diverse points of view. Via these diverse points of view you can learn to see and think about the world in ways you won't find in textbooks. My father's independence of mind often goes against the flow of the majority, and how he stays true to his own ideas influences my own sense of values and, I hope, my individuality as a writer.

My father and my mother have not only given me love; they have created memories that will warm and nourish me, always. By sharing their lives, by their mutual sympathy and support—and by weathering rough patches—they renew our family's togetherness. This is a lesson. Money cannot buy it.

# ONE BRILLIANT DAD

No such thing
as a useless dad.
No such thing
as a useless kid.

"Ah, I'm a total
waste of space!"

he says, and proves
he wants to be
a better dad.
Now is that not

one brilliant dad?

# OBSTACLES, GOALS, BLESSINGS AND HOPES

In my life so far, I've experienced any number of hardships arising from my autism. These hardships arise in turn from the fact that our society is made up of a large neurotypical majority. You'd be forgiven for assuming, then, that I feel nothing but envy toward the "normal" majority, but that's not the whole picture, not by a long shot. More and more, I've noticed the positives about having autism. Two things make this outlook possible.

The first reason is that my parents were never in a state of denial about my autism, nor did they ever consign me to a "special needs" pigeonhole. They just strove to help me get better at doing the things I was good at. Working toward independence is really important and is a necessary part of growing up for everyone, but independence—in and of itself—won't dispel or dilute autism. I attribute the ease I feel in my "autistic skin" today to my parents' unwillingness to swallow fixed ideas about autism and their resolve to provide whatever education was working the best for me at the time.

The second reason is that I've become better at making decisions for myself. Deciding things for yourself is a vital part of self-esteem. I believe that because my parents have always respected my wishes and feelings, my self-confidence had space to grow.

Whenever I hear the words "Ah, it's because he's autistic," I feel dismay. That word "autistic" packs a negative punch and this negativity, I think, corrodes the position of people with autism. For sure, functioning in our society is difficult for neuro-atypicals, but encountering difficulties is not the same thing as being unhappy. How has it come about that the word "autism" invokes pity? A part of the answer might be that we see so few role models of people living contentedly with their autism. The fact is, we have no choice but to live in a society where autism is thought of exclusively as a sorrow and a hardship—a fact that triggers further sorrow and hardship.

Even I, as a child, used to think, "Wow, if *only* I didn't have autism, wouldn't life be great?" No longer. I can't really imagine myself as not having autism because the "Myself" I'd be wouldn't be the same Myself that I am now. A Me Without Autism, even one who looked exactly the same, would have an entirely different set of ideas and way of looking at the world. Losing one's autism wouldn't be quite the same as recovering from an illness that has temporarily crippled one, for example. It isn't a case of a disease being cured or an injury being healed. It could well be that our brains are wired in different ways. People might say, "By becoming neurotypical, good things will happen and you wouldn't be such a nuisance for everyone around you," and I'm not denying that it would be a dream come true for people who have to live with autism at present. Nevertheless, how would you feel if you were obliged to undergo medical treatment for the sole reason that the person you are is an inconvenience? Not medicine to alleviate symptoms, but an operation to effect a root-and-branch change to who and what you are and remove all meaning from everything you thought was beautiful and precious?

It is unfair that even the personalities of people with autism get invalidated because of our differences from the norm. I take it as a given that if I'm no good at something, I'll have to practice at it. The tough part is when people get riled and reproach us for taking ages to learn what neurotypicals pick up effortlessly. At times like these it really feels hammered into me that I'm useless at everything. It seems to be not widely enough recognized that there are positives to be found in the neurologies of people with autism. If the world at large would take a deeper interest in how our brains work and research our uniquenesses—as opposed to focusing on our treatment and "cure"—we could take pride in our neuro-atypical natures.

I wonder, sometimes: if I didn't have autism, would I be able to interact with people who did have autism in the same way that I interacted with everybody else? Would I be able to explore the hearts and minds of those who live with such extreme difficulties and work out how to improve their quality of life?

There are reasons why people with autism exist in the world, I believe. Those who are determined to live with us and not give up on us are deeply compassionate people, and this kind of compassion must be a key to humanity's long-term survival. Even when the means of self-expression and/or intelligence are lacking, we still respond to love. Knowing we are cherished is a source of hope—and no matter how tough things get, you can always soldier on as long as there's hope. Since I came into this world, I've benefited from many wonderful experiences. Thanks to friends, family and supporters, I can be grateful for what's around me and keep a smile on my face.

Life is precious, so we try to help each other; and as someone who tends to be on the receiving end of this mutual assistance, I feel especially heartened when people stay cheerful and positive as they assist me. Every single time someone treats me with kindness, my determination to live well from tomorrow is rejuvenated. This is how I feel empowered to give something back to my family and society, even if my contribution is modest. Thanks to the people who come to me with questions and ask for my opinions about things—never mind if I can't always answer—I get to think about what I want. I feel blessed that I'm able to consider what kind of life would bring me contentment, and to exercise choices which might bring this about.

I love nature, I have an interest in letters and numbers, and I'm fascinated by some things that other people have no interest in whatsoever. If these fascinations are rooted in my autistically wired brain and if neurotypical people are unable to access these wonders, then I have to say that the immutable beauties of autism are such that I count myself lucky to be born with the condition.

Issues like our obsessions, fixations and panic attacks do

need to be worked on, but rather than moaning about problems for which there are no quick fixes, I prefer to concentrate on my self-management skills, even if progress is gradual. To live a life where I feel blessed to have autism: that will be my goal from now on.

# 79

## DEAR PARENTS

All parents, I guess, feel sadness when a child of theirs is diagnosed with autism. Because I was the child being diagnosed and not my mother or father being presented with the diagnosis, I can only imagine being the child in that situation, who has to watch his or her parents surrender to that long-term sadness. However miserable you might be about your child, please don't walk away. The child can't change what they are. They don't know why they aren't the same as other children any more than you do, but, however hard things are for you, it's harder for the child. Believe me. The child has nowhere to walk away to and you are the only people they can turn to for help. Will your child's autism wholly transform your lives, and if so, how? While I don't have the answer, there isn't much that time doesn't help with. A child with a disability has entered your life, but must that degrade your life's value? You choose how you live your life. Wherever you go, whatever you do, whatever happens to you, your essential nature stays constant, I believe. Yes, raising a child with autism can be highly demanding, but please remember, just as you worry about your child, so your child worries about you.

My own parents have never discussed my future all that

much since the time I was small, it seems. They never thought that because of my disability I had to follow such-and-such a route. Thanks to that, for better or for worse, here I am, as I am. Your child, too, will one day be an adult. For them to live life with the same degree of independence as neurotypical offspring might be difficult, but one day your child-rearing, child-minding days will come to an end. Parents grow older until they can no longer look after their adult children. The period in which we are together as parents and child is finite. So please, while the child still *is* a child, and while you're still around to do so, support them well. Laugh together and share your stories. You won't be revisiting these years. Value them. That's all I'd ask.

# 80

## MOTHER'S DAY 2013

Sometimes I go out with my special needs helper to a local supermarket. To practice shopping, I buy my own snacks. Today, in the corner of the food section, I saw they were selling bunches of red carnations for Mother's Day. I thought, *I'd like to buy some for Mom.* But, of course, I wasn't able simply to vocalize this thought because it's so hard for me to tell others what I want via speech or gestures. On this occasion, however, I managed to produce this two-word line: "Carnation . . . Buy." My helper was pretty gob-smacked! Here's how I pulled it off. First, I replayed a "memory clip" of carnations in my head. By viewing this clip, I was able to say the word "carnation." Next, to access the verb I needed to go with the flower, I directed my thoughts to what I was doing at the time. Words like "walk," "see" and "think" floated through my mind, but then, the fact of our being in a supermarket unveiled the word "buy." That verb was the best fit for the word "carnation" and by combining the two I got "Carnation . . . Buy." Once there, I was free to think, *That's what I need to say!* and—finally— I said it.

I only had enough coins with me for a single flower, but when we came home and I gave the carnation to Mom, she was elated. I'm still not good at the practical aspects of buy-ing things without assistance, but it was fantastic that I could tell my helper what I wanted to buy. And I'm still a long way from being able to speak in this way whenever I want to. I know now, though, that there are times when, in a pinch, I can pull it off. Giving flowers to my mom on Mother's Day was a dream I'd been harboring for years. Today, one red carnation in a room at home did all my talk-ing for me.

# AFTERWORD

The communication methods that I, with my severe autism, have used so far in my life are "hand-supported" writing, letter-tracing on the palm of a transcriber and, these days, independent pointing at the letters on an alphabet grid. The first—the hand-supported writing—involves writing on paper with a pen while an assistant is lightly cupping the back of the writer's hand to help keep him or her on task. Letter-tracing is not dissimilar, but here I trace the letters onto the open palm of a transcriber rather than onto paper. These days I use the alphabet-grid method—without anyone's help and without any physical contact—to express my thoughts and feelings. My alphabet grid resembles a standard QWERTY keyboard, with the letters and numbers written onto a card. Recently I've become able to vocalize the characters as I spell out words by touching them in the right order with my index finger. For creative writing, I switch to my computer. My alphabet grid is best for on-the-spot verbal communication, because when I use the computer I can get sidetracked by typing in whatever words pop into my head, or by its phonetic alphabet-to-Chinese character (*hiragana* to *kanji*) converter. There have been times

205

when the person I'm communicating with has been left waiting for ages.

Until quite recently it was said that people who have severe autism could never express themselves. So a number of people might have been surprised to see me setting out my thoughts via the alphabet grid and computer. As I've been conveying the story of my inner life to the wider world I've learned that many people—both with autism and without—find that my writing strikes a chord with their own experiences. What is this common chord? The answer, I think, is to do with those emotions that crush us all. Evolution appears to have resulted in the mastery of reason over what we say and what we do, but in reality, it's rare for our minds and hearts to be wholly rational and stable. We fret over how best to tame our feelings and attain a state of equilibrium. By translating our states of mind into words, perhaps we can better grasp the reasons that underlie our insecurity. To live a positive life, understanding and acceptance are key. We all seek the courage to stand up again after falling down. It would mean the world to me if this book could occasionally serve as a gentle nudge in the right direction.

NAOKI HIGASHIDA
*Japan, 2015*

## ABOUT THE AUTHOR

NAOKI HIGASHIDA was born in Kimitsu, Japan, in 1992. Diagnosed with severe autism when he was five, he subsequently learned to communicate using a handmade alphabet grid and began to write poems and short stories. At the age of thirteen he wrote *The Reason I Jump*, which was published in Japan in 2007. Its English translation came out in 2013, and it has now been published in more than thirty languages. Higashida has since published several books in Japan, including children's and picture books, poems, and essays. The subject of an award-winning Japanese television documentary in 2014, he continues to give presentations throughout the country about his experience of autism.

## ABOUT THE TRANSLATORS

DAVID MITCHELL is the author of seven novels, including *Cloud Atlas, The Bone Clocks,* and, most recently, *Slade House.* KA YOSHIDA was born in Yamaguchi, Japan, and specialized in English poetry at Notre Dame Seishin University. KA Yoshida and David Mitchell live in Ireland with their two children.

ABOUT THE TYPE

This book was set in Fairfield, the first typeface from the hand of the distinguished American artist and engraver Rudolph Ruzicka (1883–1978). Ruzicka was born in Bohemia (in the present-day Czech Republic) and came to America in 1894. He set up his own shop, devoted to wood engraving and printing, in New York in 1913 after a varied career working as a wood engraver, in photoengraving and banknote printing plants, and as an art director and freelance artist. He designed and illustrated many books, and was the creator of a considerable list of individual prints—wood engravings, line engravings on copper, and aquatints.